GLAD YOU Asked!

A COLLECTION OF QUESTIONS TO ASK YOUR CHILDREN

RUTH ANN MILLER

For additional copies, contact:
Gospel Express Ministries
P.O. Box 217
Lynn, NC 28750

Or visit gospelexpress.com

Photography by:
Paige Schlabach Photography
Tiffany Reif Photography
Deborah Isabel Borkholder
Sheila Nolt Photography

Qr Code Footage:
New Horizon Studios
Gospel Express Studios
Berlin Gardens Studio
Schlabach Printers

Layout and printing by:

Sugarcreek, OH
schlabachprinters.com

Acknowledgments

I am so grateful to the Mighty Counselor who is the author of all good ideas, life, comfort, and creativity, and is our source of power to carry them out.

To my kind husband and children whose release, support, input, investments, and encouragement was vital for me to be able to turn these ideas into a printed tool. I have learned a lot and felt so cared for by the good questions you all take time to ask me! I am especially indebted to our darling daughter, Grace, whose skilled hands cheerfully served in extra domestics in order to extend my writing time, and the extra time and expertise given by Dave, Derek, and Deborah to this book.

This project would not be what it is without the empowerment from the Gospel Express Team and Board and my dedicated, inspiring book coach and editor, Janessa Miller.

Credits and appreciation to Dr. Nic Miller and our adult children; Derek, Eugene, Kyle and Grace for the bonus teaching videos available throughout the book via QR codes.

Lastly, in heartfelt appreciation, I'd like to rain down shimmering confetti over all of you friends, parents, and children who asked about, prayed for, previewed, gave feedback, posed for photos, encouraged me, or contributed to this project in so many ways!!

Table of Contents

Elementary, Ages 6–10

Middle School, Ages 11–14

Index Parent Helps

How to Use This Book

Your Position

This section suggests specific adjustments in your parenting mentality and methods as your child matures that may be needed to maintain a healthy relationship for both of your sakes.

Our Story

This section includes snapshots into our own failures, tests, learning curves, and victories as we raised our five children. We hope it is an encouragement that you are not alone in your battles and a reminder of the rewards of staying emotionally connected to your children, grandchildren, and other children who need a loving, stable grown-up to walk with them through life.

Your Own Heart Care

You also have feelings and needs as a parent, grandparent, or mentor, and your inner care is important. This section is to prepare you for how this specific date subject might affect you, the grown-up, and have you ponder what might be going on in your heart. Processing our childhood and how it affected our thinking in specific areas helps us stay in touch with why we think the way we do, why we are who we are, and ultimately helps us be more understanding to the child we are listening to.

What Can I Do?

The goal here is to remind you of the power of your influence. Far-reaching fruits can come out of your personal involvement and kind responses to difficulties your child may be experiencing. Here I try to offer specific ideas we gleaned from others that helped us in our parenting trials.

Before the Date

Here I quickly mention any blanks you may want to pencil in before you leave for the date in the closing prayer or spoken blessing sections. I may also suggest an example out of your own life you may be able to bring out to make these specific questions a more relatable conversation with your child.

I hope on this date

In a nutshell, I share the goal and purpose of the specific subject and intentional questions curated for this date.

Offense Check

Because life happens and we are not perfect, this is to clear up anything between your child and you that could hinder either one of you from fully engaging, enjoying, and opening up your hearts to each other.

Questions

On each date, there are ten intentional questions on the

theme subject to learn more about that specific area of your child's life. There are also a few random, fun questions sprinkled in for you to use whenever is most fitting to lighten things up, but these have nothing to do with the theme subject.

Closing Prayer or Spoken Blessing

We have found that voicing gratitude, speaking life into or praying over a child, and voicing their positive attributes is a meaningful and life-giving way to end your one-on-one time together. The samples are only there for you if you need ideas. I do encourage you to speak what comes natural and seems fitting to you at the time.

Where to Go for Your Dates?

You can choose an economical location such as backyard swings, a ride along to the local hardware store, bike rides, camping, hiking trails, fishing ponds, tubing, paddleboarding, or ice-cream or cupcake shops. Or you can go as extravagant as traveling to the city to visit unique places like a LEGO store, Cabela's, clay pigeon shoots, batting cages, hitting ranges, rodeos, museums, fairs, theme parks, the zoo, the Ark, or even spending the night somewhere.

Sometimes rides to and from school, sports, music lessons, dental or optometrist appointments, etc. are perfect and less intimidating to casually discuss or ask some of these questions, either from looking over them ahead or actually getting the book and one of you reading them out loud to discuss.

Another idea is to honor the child by giving them a choice of where they would enjoy going. Children in certain birth orders can tend to be frequently outvoted in their desired places to eat or to go, by adults or other siblings. The offer for them to choose where to go may actually be a huge part of them remembering the date with fondness all their life. Obviously you may want to mention ahead any distance, expense, or time limitations that need to apply to their choices. Reminding them of the need for a semi-private place for a quiet, uninterrupted conversation may help them weed out noisy, active places. Examples would include choosing a booth instead of a table or a quiet park bench away from busy streets and sidewalks.

Another good time in a child's life to accomplish a memorable time away is to plan a mother/daughter or father/son overnight getaway for bat mitzvah or bat barakah when they are going into adulthood from eleven to twelve years old.

We trust you as parents or grandparents are formulating your own family traditions as they transition into adulthood.

One idea we used was to present a framed print out of my husband's spoken blessing, including their name and its meaning at each of our children's graduation parties. This visual on their room wall served as a continual reminder of their purpose, worth, and destiny.

Calendar

This is a reminder note at the end of each date to check off in our table of contents which date you took and at which age level. If you turn back to our index calendar you can not only keep a record of the specifics dates you took, but when you took them and with which child and proceed to pencil in goals for your next dates.

Why I Wrote This Book

Easy and Fast

My goal for this date tool is that you can pick it up and use it whether you are a reader or not. Whether you are a mom or dad, grandparent, or investing your personal time in some other form of children's ministry as a teacher, therapist, or mentor.

Mind Prep Minute

There are short parent tips before each date subject you can quickly browse over in a minute to prepare your heart to engage with your child, whether in a car line at school or on an intentional ice-cream date. I have attempted to do the work for you so you can connect on a heart-to-heart level, stay updated on their life, take care of necessary, preventive maintenance, and have fun doing it!

Seizing Your Privilege

This is to assist you to do shepherding well amid all your other pressures. A way to help you ask the meaningful, crucial questions that need to be discussed as well as the adventurous and silly ones we sprinkled throughout for fun.

Stay Connected

This book is loaded with questions I longed for my parents to ask me when I was younger, questions that would have helped us bond and helped them get to know the real me.

Get Personal

Questions that will help parents understand, build up, and train each child "in the way they should go" as individuals.

Be Their Counselor

Questions that can help prevent rejection, shame, guilt, bitterness, insecurities, and long-term relationship triggers that tend to be carried into our adult lives and marriages if not processed while they are happening.

Being a Safe Person

When a child is welcomed to share the hard things weighing on their heart with a trusted adult who can offer them a healthy perspective on the circumstance, it can prevent lies from taking root.

Keep Your Spot

In many cases, schoolteachers, youth leaders, spouses, pastors, caretakers, and counselors later end up taking a parents' privileged place of processing a person's past to help them become more whole. Most insecurity and fear "filters" can be resolved quickly and more easily if dealt with in an up-to-date manner during our childhood.

Ongoing Stability

Accountability is another huge preventive maintenance

just like an oil change or servicing your car. What large, close-knit families in small homes used to offer is no longer happening with latchkey kids with one parent or independent-minded families in larger homes with more private rooms and separate vehicles. My hope is that the accountability of a child knowing they will be asked about their personal thought life, viewing habits, trials, and temptations could stop their small failures from becoming lifelong, devastating addictions. Your personal involvement, interest, and questions weekly or monthly can make all the difference, one child at a time!

You Matter

I have found it to be true that unless I process my past and try to find healing, there may be walls around my heart that affect how openly I can give and receive love to and from my spouse and children.

If a parent has lacked affirmation during their childhood, that constant longing and void of rest in who they are can result in self-centeredness in marriage and parenting. When we live in a "not good enough" or "less than" mentality, it is very difficult to offer positive words of affirmation and gratitude to our children.

But thanks be to God, we can rise above by His grace and stop that vicious cycle and start a safe, loving, affirming culture of honor in our homes!

My faith was boosted and I was so delighted lately to observe in an extended family reunion that my generation of parents, through seeking and knowing Jesus, have stopped the generational cycle of disconnect, rejection, and shame their parents had battled. I saw before me a transformed generation with peaceful, loving homes and heart-to-heart connections with their children. That is who Jesus is and what He gladly does when invited into our lives and families.

I am not the same girl my husband married thirty years ago, not even the same woman who raised our young children. I am enjoying greater wholeness as I sway in a hammock of Grace during my fifties. I expect I will be at an even healthier place if you ask me in another decade. That is why I inserted "Your Own Heart Care" sections in the "Parent Tip" section for you to ponder and care for your own state of being during every season of your children's lives. It makes for a life rich with relational fulfillment that absorbs the jostling that our aging vessels want to crack under at times.

My slogan for this kind of close-up connection with your children as they grow into adults is "Smile kindly when they tell you terrible things." Remember your own childish ways and life as a youth.

What We Don't Want

We are not promoting a "child-focused parenting" where the children manipulate and control. We endeavor for these conversations to bring connectedness along with daily teaching, training, and gentle, self-controlled, loving punishment for disobedience. Our goal is to help you avoid a "rules without relationship" kind of parenting.

This tool is geared toward hearing each other's hearts and should first be practiced between the parents or spouses. Cultivated out of that unity, we hope the home becomes a safe, trusted place for children to be obedient yet honest and treat each other with honor.

PRESCHOOL

AGES 3–5

POSITION OF ADULT ROLE:

Activating conscience for a lifetime on what is right and wrong, safe and unsafe, acceptable and unacceptable. Creating clear boundaries on who is in charge with loving gentleness and firm maturity.

Date 1:
Creating a Safe Culture

Our Story

My mind goes back to an evening bath time when I had a preschooler of my own. As I knelt over the steaming tub, reaching for shampoo with one hand and cradling my three-year-old's darling head with the other, I washed the soft layers of my daughter's hair. After sitting back up, she studied her toes and said softly, "Mom, I have ish-thues again." I smiled at her pronunciation. Surely a preschooler's issues could be solved without too much stress.

Creating a Culture

My daughter's natural instinct was to use this time with me to share secrets that were bothering her. When we were not in a rush, I would occasionally ask if there was anything the children wanted to talk about during bath or bedtime routines. It became a safe time to share what was bothering their little hearts.

Whether you grew up in a safe environment or not, you can create a safe culture with your children starting today. It is a gift to take time out of your pressing schedule and focus your love and attention on the unique little person that is your child.

My husband and I are grateful to have experienced much grace for our own personal issues by tapping into God's healing. As young parents, Dave and I had only been Christians for a few years with three children we were trying to raise. We were zealous in faith but broken and needy inside. There were times our children made themselves vulnerable with us and were left feeling unsafe as we had sometimes felt with our own parents.

We began to understand Heaven's love and interest in our lives through taking in the Word and some good teaching. Although we couldn't fathom why or how our Heavenly Father could know and care for us so personally, the new understanding prompted us to consider how we were relating to our children with more intention. Did our children ever feel unsafe with us?

We began seeing areas where we had not been as intentional as we had hoped. At times we still parented out of self-centered, surface-level motivations. It felt difficult not to be encumbered by the physical and mental demands of running and providing for a home.

What Can I Do?

We learned to watch the faces and eyes of our children in moments of correction. By watching their reactions, we can catch when there is hurt, shame, or misunderstanding that goes deeper than healthy correction should cause. A child will learn to shut down to protect themselves from hurting again in hurt or shame, and many children carry these misguided tools into adulthood.

With God's help, we attempted to create more inviting moments for our children to open their hearts to us. We did a lot of apologizing when we missed the mark, disciplined in anger, raised our voices, or spoke harshly as young parents. Thank God, children are so kind and forgiving if we just ask!

I love how we as parents can set the tone in our homes and offer our child words at a young age to help them express the positive and negative emotions they experience. We can let them know we care about how they feel while making them aware that they still need to obey, even when it feels hard. You are training them to learn to be aware of what they feel and then rise to an appropriate response.

We can be on the offense by teaching our children how to openly recognize emotions they are feeling, instead of stuffing them. Emotions can be expressed and validated without being given control of our decisions. Hopefully, we are molding children into responsible yet sensitive adults that will excel in relationships, communicating better because they are aware of others' needs as well as their own. Before we

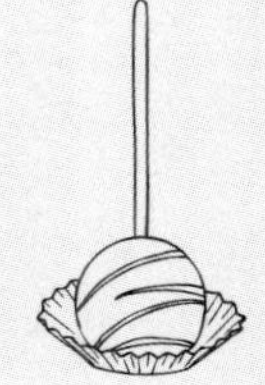

look at your child on this date, it may be important for you to look inward at the kind of culture you have formed between yourself and your child.

Your Own Heart Care

As I experienced a beautiful, close relationship with our children, I learned to stop and grieve the fact that I didn't have that kind of relationship with my own parents growing up. Experiencing the Heavenly Father's unconditional love enables and motivates us to create a culture of relationships that are not based on performance. Our gentle

Holy Father is safe, and our desire is that all children experience that kind of acceptance.

1. Are there lies or habits of thinking embedded in your own identity that are keeping you from connecting with your child?

2. Can you freely give what you never had by extending grace to your parents and humbly receiving the gifts that God has so freely given to you?

Before the Date

You can pencil the words of your choice in each blank of the spoken blessing offered at the end of the date questions. Doing it ahead of time will help you avoid unnecessary long pauses while you are with them.

I Hope This Date:

1. Will help you gauge both how easily your child opens up with your individual attention and how safe your child feels to be vulnerable with you.

2. Will free your child up with an opportunity to speak about anything that they experienced or are feeling that they may not have had the courage or opportunity to bring up before now.

Date Questions

- What is your favorite game to play?

1. Who do you like to go tell when you get hurt?
2. Who in your life smiles at you the most?
3. When someone smiles at you, how does that make you feel?
4. Has anything sad happened lately?
5. Do we sometimes say things that do not seem kind to you?
6. Were you ever scared of me?
7. Is there anyone that you feel scared to be with?
8. Do you think everyone in our family is treated kindly?
9. Do you feel like I take time just to watch you play and be with you?
10. Has anyone ever done something to hurt you that you want to talk about?

- Do you know what Daddy does at work?
- Do you know the name of our president?
- Listen carefully. What are some sounds you can hear right now?

Closing Question:

Now, is there anything you want to ask me?

Testimony Video

Spoken Blessing

Face your child and make eye contact as you gently speak this blessing out loud.

Two things that I really like about you are:
The way you often (2 verb phrases) _____________ and _____________.

I also really enjoy (activity) _____________ with you when I am home.

I like taking you along when we go away to _____________ together. I like making memories together. I am so glad God gave you to us!

As your (who you are to them) _____________, I want to speak good health and safety over you and pray you will have fun learning many new things as you grow this year in Jesus's name!

Schedule

Take time to look at your next month's schedule, discuss with your child the next possible date, and pencil it in the index calendar as well as your planner or phone calendar.

Responses to Remember

Routines and Relationships

Our Story

Miniature desks lined the sunny walls of our quaint home-school room, each topped with a colorful stack of books. It was the official opening morning of The Discipleship and Academics Family Homeschool, and my children excitedly began opening their stiff new covers. What I didn't know was that I would embark on my first homeschooling hurdle immediately.

Our bright, active toddler was experiencing the newness of our gathering place for the first time along with the rest of us. He alternated between siblings, pulling himself up by each chair with his sweet baby face, straining to see what was on their desks, and continually disrupting my dreamy orderly first day of school. Drumming up my cheeriest voice, I beckoned him to the door, saying he may now go out in the living room to play! All of you experienced adults can laugh with me, knowing well the living room and its familiar toys held no interest while the rest of us gathered inside this mysterious new room together.

As I followed him out, preparing to close the door behind him, a thought came to me suddenly. *"This child will negatively associate school with rejection if he is asked to leave us and be alone whenever we are doing school books."* It was like the Lord gave me a warning and a solution all at once. My mind chimed *Aha!* and I acted on the revelation. Finding a little table and chair, I formed our toddler his own "school desk" in that tiny study room. I assigned some preschool activity pages for him to finish while the others studied and soon ordered his own little Pre-K curriculum set, which arrived at our door later that week.

What Can I Do?

The key to all good people skills is to put ourselves in their shoes and do to them as we would have them do to us (Matt. 7:12). Following this principle will prevent a lot of us parents from provoking our children to wrath (Eph. 6:4). Instead of being pushed out of the school room, our toddler now had a mini desk and chair in line with the other desks where he was "required" to sit and complete his assigned pages. I smiled as he begged to go to the living room for a break, which I only permitted after he had finished a page in one of his school books. God is genius.

What are your frustrating scenarios with your child or others in the home at the moment? Have you asked the God of all wisdom what to do? Watch for the idea. He uses a variety of ways to answer. It may be through a thought, people, or circumstances. He answers our seeking. "Every good and every perfect gift comes from above" (James 1:17, KJV).

Before the Date

During this date with your child, ask God to help you see your home life habits and routines through the lens of this young one's experience. <u>If your preschool child is the youngest</u>, they may very likely be dealing with feelings of rejection from being treated as a source of irritation to older children's projects.

<u>If your child has a younger toddler sibling</u>, they may desire for you to respect their needs by providing specific times for noninvasive play. Simultaneously, you can encourage them to look at it as a privilege to teach the baby to play by allowing the toddler in their play area at other times. Try to put yourself in your child's shoes. How do they experience their siblings most of the time? What stresses them and causes them to react negatively? Is there a way you can make their waking up or going to bed more affirming and memorable?

Sometimes older children's schedules or jobs tend to take dominion, or life is very revolved around the baby's needs. The middle children can begin to believe they are only tagalongs to more important events and siblings.

What small changes could really make this young one feel understood and wanted? You don't need to allow the child to manipulate your schedule or become self-centered. When I listened to the Heroes of Faith series audiobook on Susanna Wesley (IBLP Publications, 2005), I learned that not only did she use her apron over her head as her prayer escape, but she determined to have a certain day of the week where she spent some increment of time individually with each child. Goals. I was challenged by how Susanna raised and educated their ten children (out of the nineteen she bore that survived infancy) on a meager income while her husband was preaching the gospel and writing sermons, poetry, and hymns while away from home much of the time.

Sometimes whining, negativity, or ingratitude can be caused by feeling overlooked. A child may feel they are not worth one-on-one time with the parent because of other children or priorities "screaming louder" for attention. You can initiate a simple time together by holding them, sharing story time alone, or pushing them on the swing. Some conversation with no one else around pulling your attention can make them feel loved and secure enough to cause a shift in their attitude.

Date Questions

🥤 Which farm animal is your favorite?

1. Who do you really enjoy playing with in our family?
2. Do you feel angry inside your heart at anybody?
3. Who do you like to cuddle with?
4. What do you like about mornings?
5. Do you like bedtimes?
6. Is there anybody's house you don't like going to? Why is that?
7. Is anyone so mean to you that you would just want to run away from them?
8. Do you think Jesus wants you to hide your toys or share them with others?
9. Has anything happened to you that I should know about?
10. Have you been trying to share and be patient and kind with others?

🥤 Which of your shoes are your favorite and why?

🥤 What is one of your favorite songs?

🥤 Where is your favorite place to be in water when it is warm outside?

Closing question

Now, is there anything you want to ask me?

Spoken Blessing

Praying out loud to God over your child can help them become more comfortable in His presence.

Father God, thank you for how you made __________ (child's name). Would you please give _____________ a gentle, kind heart of giving for others, even when others are not always gentle, kind, thoughtful, or sharing with them? God, please help ________ to forgive as you forgave the people who were mean to you. Jesus, we know people said mean things to you when you were on the earth. Soldiers even whipped you and hammered nails into your hands when they put you on that wooden cross. Help us to forgive people like you do.

Adult question to child: Would you be willing to follow me in a prayer to God for those who have not been kind to you?

Adult lead the child in two prayers:

1. God, will you put kindness and gentleness in the heart of ___________ so (he or she) doesn't keep hurting or bossing others.

Parent: fill in the blanks with any specific hardships the child mentioned on this date.

2. God, please heal my heart and help me to keep forgiving _________. Thank you, Jesus, that you let the soldiers put those sharp nails in your hands and feet for all my sins and you still forgave them.

Schedule

Take time to look at your next month's schedule, discuss with your child the next possible date, and pencil it in the index calendar as well as your planner or phone calendar.

Responses to Remember

Date 3:
Maintaining a Clear Conscience

Our Story

During our bedtime routine one evening, one of my children took advantage of having me alone and asked if we could talk. Her little hands and feet fidgeted as she slowly laid out the event that had been bothering her conscience.

One Sunday, we had been visitors at a church gathering held in a school. Our daughter had only a short amount of time to play with her friend there, and while playing side by side as little girls do, they had entered the ladies' restroom. The friend proceeded to drop a pen into the toilet and flushed it straight down the drain. Although innocent enough, the confession made me cringe at the potential of teachers racing over a clogged pipe during the following school day and the unnecessary frustration of a plumber searching for the problematic source.

My daughter did not have to mastermind the idea or be the pen-flusher herself to feel the guilt of their actions. She was present and felt her participation. Witnessing and partaking in another's actions, which she knew to be wrong, left my daughter with a guilty conscience, and she came to me seeking relief and forgiveness.

Creating a Culture

Whether it's their own actions or others' deeds, we want our children to learn a lifestyle of keeping a clear conscience daily before God, including peers' ideas that they could be engaging with inappropriately.

If they share something that seems very inappropriate with you, remember that curiosity is innocent learning and should never be shamed. Children are innocent until they have been told or educated on why something is not acceptable. They need your guidance. This is your opportunity to take time to gently teach this child what is right and wrong, appropriate or not, without shaming them.

Before the Date

If the child confesses something shameful that bothers their conscience, no matter how minuscule or substantial, remember to respond kindly and take time to lead them in a prayer of confession. Name the sin to God out loud and ask God to please forgive them in order to clear their conscience of the offense.

You are helping this child learn that guilt can be a kind reminder to come to God for forgiveness and cleansing. As you learn to approach this in a way that feels safe, it will create a bonding experience for you and your child. This early foundation will open the door for them to feel welcome to come to you for the rest of their life with big and small issues.

A Note on Discipline

Loving discipline should only be used for direct disobedience to a clear instruction, not for failure to perform well.

We want to be very careful in giving punishment as a result of honest confessions, lest we communicate that it is better for future failures and sins to be kept secret from parents. In life, your child will naturally reap the consequences of what they have sown. We want to encourage voluntary, honest confessions by first listening very kindly and affirming our unconditional love for them before any negative consequences are applied. This will invite your child back to you as a future source to clear their conscience of an offense or secret sin versus stuffing it down or going to a peer about it.

A direct consequence associated with the offense can teach a lesson as long as affirmation and gratitude for honesty are first expressed to the child. Remember how your Heavenly Father responds to your confession of sins. Natural consequences of reaping may be, and often are, a result of sinful actions, but mercy flows from God to us in forgiveness when we are repentant.

If a child has confessed any wrong behavior done to them, you can discern the proper next steps using Jesus's model for relationship problems in Matthew 18:15–16 (NKJV):

> Moreover if your brother sins against you, go and tell him his fault between you and him alone. If he hears you, you have gained your brother. But if he will not hear, take with you one or two more, that "by the mouth of two or three witnesses every word may be established."

Discern whether any circumstance your child shared about is serious enough to have them go with you to talk to the other party involved. If yes, offer to go with your young child to ask for forgiveness. If another child is involved, one of their parents could be present as well. Ask God to show you your motive for approaching the other child or parent and make sure you have the Lord's peace after praying about it. Any feelings of accusation sensed from the other party can cause more relationship problems than the incident itself.

Your Own Heart Care

Is there anything bothering your conscience that you should be confessing to God or anyone else? You want to teach this concept with freedom and confidence because of your own obedience in this principle.

Personal Reflections

I hope on this date:

1. You kindly activate this child's conscience for a lifetime on what is respectful and what is not without making them feel guilty.
2. You experience the joy of helping your child find and learn how to keep a peace of mind that will help them experience a bright, carefree, happy childhood.

Date Questions

🥤 What is your favorite snack?

1. Have you ever taken something that wasn't yours from someone and never told them?

2. Has anyone ever made you feel embarrassed or sad?

3. Your underwear area is private. Has anyone ever been disrespectful to you by asking to put down your underwear to see your private area?

4. Have you ever seen anyone else's privates?

5. Have you done anything *with* someone while playing that might not have been very respectful?

   Where would you enjoy going for vacation?

6. Have you seen any pictures or movies that bother you?

7. Is there anyone's house you do not like to go to?

   What do you like about winter?

8. Have you ever been mean to a baby or someone smaller than you?

9. Do you have any other secrets or anything bothering you that we should talk to God about?

🥤 What do you like about summer when it's warm outside?

🥤 Would you rather go sledding in the snow, boating on a lake, or horse riding someday?

Closing question

Now, is there anything you want to ask me?

Speaking Love to your Child

I am grateful God brought you into my life and that I was able to spend this time alone with you. My goal is always to be here for you in the hard times and fun times of life! I want you to feel safe telling me things you are even scared to tell me. I am your ______, and I love and care about what happens to you. Do you feel safe to come to me with anything that is bothering you?

Schedule

Take time to look at your next month's schedule, discuss with your child the next possible date, and pencil it in the index calendar as well as your planner or phone calendar.

Responses to Remember

Date 4:

Skills to Steward

Our Story

I remember the *aha!* moment when my preschool-aged son unloaded the cups from the dishwasher and placed them all neatly in rows. Each handle was perfectly angled in the same direction, and I realized this child had been given a natural skill of organization and attention to detail.

The all-inclusive family concept, even in work, creates a feeling of being needed and wanted. Although it made for wet shirts and large puddles on both my counters and floors, I would often have a washer, rinser, and dryer of dishes lined up on step stools. With rolled-up sleeves and mini Lowes carpenter aprons, they fulfilled their kitchen duty while singing, having random discussions, or hearing my instructions on how to help. Placing yet another stool for my preschooler, I would often set the clean silverware crate from the dishwasher onto the already mostly blocked counter by the silverware drawer for my three-year-old to put the silverware in their proper places.

Some preschool-appropriate chores include:

- Leaving smaller garments or washcloths for the preschooler to get out of the dryer and put into a wash basket

- Digging up and pulling weeds

- Watering plants

- Lining up Matchbox cars, stuffed animals, or shoes

- Emptying small waste cans

- Dusting

- Keeping the landscaping, decks, and driveway clean by picking up tiny branches and leaves outside

- Setting tables

- Handing Mom the eggs or learning to crack them

- Pouring ingredients into a bowl

- Washing off cupboards

- Lint-rolling carpets

Personal Reflections

I hope on this date:

1. You take time to ponder the natural skills that even your three-year-old has been given.
2. You get ideas on how to strengthen and engage your child as an asset to your home and to others in the future.
3. You consider your household routines through the eyes of your child and make any positive adjustments that will help them feel included, needed, and valued.

God created humans with a need to have purpose and accomplish exploits. Like adults, children who are given opportunities to be creative and feel productive are happier and demonstrate less signs of feeling unfulfilled through crankiness and unnecessary drama. Even the youngest child feels a sense of worth and purpose when they feel needed and are able to achieve a task.

During this date, study your child to discover what they enjoy doing or maybe would like to try helping out within your home routines.

Date Questions

1. What job would you want when you get bigger?
2. What are some things you think you are good at doing?
3. What are a few jobs you hope you can help out with here at home when you get a little older?
4. Would you rather play indoors or outside?
5. Would you rather make a birthday gift for Grandma or go buy one?
6. Would you rather look at books or play catch?
7. Is it more fun for you to help me pull weeds and plant and water seeds or for me to help you catch butterflies and bugs?
8. Does it upset you more when a room is messy or when you have no one to play with?
9. Would you rather draw pictures for me or listen to me read a story?
10. Would you rather build something new by yourself with LEGO® bricks or see how well you can hit the bucket to throw them all back in?

- Can you name some things that fly in the sky?
- What would you enjoy doing with me sometime next week if I am not busy?
- What animals have you ever petted or held?

Closing question:

Now, is there anything you want to ask me?

Testimony Video

Spoken Blessing

Smiling and looking into their face, speak these or your own words to your child.

I have noticed that you have done a good job of helping at home by_______________ and ________________. Sometimes you even offer to______________. We are grateful for how you are willing to ______________ when we ask you even if you would rather______________. This makes our job as parents easier. I think soon you can maybe even do some ______________ as you grow older. You enjoy ______________, don't you? When we go to stores and you don't ______________, this is very helpful to us. Thank you for being a good helper by______________ when we go away. I love you and am thankful God gave you to us.

Schedule

Take time to look at your next month's schedule, discuss with your child the next possible date, and pencil it in the index calendar as well as your planner or phone calendar.

Responses to Remember

Date 5:

Personality

Our Story

Whether journaling, grabbing photos or video footage of everyday life at home, or capturing special occasions, every memory becomes priceless. Jotted-down notes of my children's words, comments, or actions when they were younger have become favorite treasures to laugh about now. Some of our favorite family quotes come from watching home videos that lead to our children quoting each other when they were still in single-digit ages.

When our adult son comes home from his secondary job painting fences, we laughingly quote his proud little four-year-old voice, squealing, "Hey, look! I got paint on my face; my mom painted it!" I smile as I recognize and remember that there was a project-oriented man in him even as a little preschooler.

What Can I Do?

One of the greatest gifts you can give your adult children is a creation of their childhood memories. This could look like compiling videos on your phone or creating photo books from different years of your life. We have converted our Hi8 video footage of their childhood days into DVDs to pop in and watch, as well as a personal photo book I presented to each one at their graduation. We laugh at how scared they all were to see what photos their mother might have included before they got to open them.

Once our children start dating, we often watch home video footage during a visit with their significant other. Watching each other's home videos helps a dating couple observe and understand who their significant other is and how some of it already showed through when they were very young. Some memories are painful or embarrassing, but most of it is cute, edifying, interesting, and hilarious. I remind you in this preschool age to capture precious childhood moments, the adorable and the difficult, as well as writing down cute things they say—you really won't remember if you don't!

Your Family

As you think about the little people in your house, remind yourself that they are individually different. Try to remain in this mindset and seek God for His wisdom to help shape each individual into who He created and meant for them to be in your family and, someday, in society.

Down through the years, people have studied the various personality types using different methods. There are many choices to help you identify individuals' strengths and weaknesses in order to understand and appreciate each person more completely. We will name some of the most used terminologies and tests available at older ages. At this early age, it may be most helpful to simply observe your child's tendencies without labeling them.

Personal Reflections

I hope on this date:

You are inspired to study your child so you can help instill a balanced view of humility and gratefulness to God for how He created them, without comparing in a proud or negative light to others.

If you have time, fill in the sample of a cherished memory (below the date questions) before you go on the date. It will help you in sharing one meaningful, specific thing they would be encouraged to hear about when you are with them.

Date Questions

What is one of your favorite songs?

1. If we had a birthday party for you, would you rather have one friend come or a bunch of them?

2. Do you like it when a lot of people are laughing and talking at the same time, or does it get too loud?

3. Do you like knowing our plan for the day in the morning, or is it fun to be surprised?

What makes you laugh?

4. Would you rather go to Grandma's house and help her with her work or have her come sit in your room while you show her your stuff?

What is your favorite lunch?

5. Would you rather be really smart or very funny or always kind?

6. Do you like when people come to our house?

7. Do you like when we stay home and play with you or when we all go away together?

8. Would you rather pick up all the toys in your room by yourself and get a prize or have me help you pick them up?

Who would you want to be like when you get older?

9. Do you like when children follow you and you can tell them what to do, or would you rather someone else decides what to play and leads out?

What are some things that swim in the water?

10. What would you want to do together next before I have to go back to work?

Parent: If they can't think of something to do right then, you can offer some ideas of your own like going on a walk, giving a piggyback ride, counting as far as your child can, pushing them on a swing, reading a story, or singing while you rock your child.

Closing question:

Now, is there anything you want to ask me?

Cherish Memories Out Loud

I remember when you were a baby, you had __________ hair, and your fingers and toes were so __________, and you would get all excited when__________. I loved to try to get you to smile or coo by __________. Sometimes we would lay you on the __________ in the __________. At first, you may have been scared when __________. A few gifts I remember that people gave you were __________. When you were getting new teeth, you would __________. Your favorite way to go to sleep would be __________. When you woke up, you would usually __________. I love how God made you!

Schedule

Take time to look at your next month's schedule, discuss with your child the next possible date, and pencil it in the index calendar as well as your planner or phone calendar.

Responses to Remember

Date 6:

Love Language

Your Heart

Have you ever experienced someone going out of their way to do a thoughtful act of kindness, but it's really not your thing? You would never be so rude as to tell them in the moment, so you show due gratitude. Likewise, you have probably experienced investing thought, money, or effort into loving someone only to feel like they barely noticed or appreciated it.

Most of us benefit from being aware of what our main Love Languages™ are in order to help ourselves and our families understand each other. Instead of blaming those around us for not being loving, we can then communicate the specific ways we do feel more loved. Doing so can increase our understanding of why we may feel deficiencies in certain categories of care.

In his book *The 5 Love Languages: The Secret to Love that Lasts*, Dr. Gary Chapman shares how after twenty years of counseling couples he realized people had varying ways in which they actually feel and show love. By learning the five main categories we use to express love, we can more intentionally and efficiently show our love in a way that will best be received by that individual.

Gary Chapman's Five Love Languages™ are:

- ◆ Acts of Service™
- ◆ Receiving Gifts™
- ◆ Physical Touch™
- ◆ Words of Affirmation™
- ◆ Quality Time™

Our Story

In the last decade, our adult children have been involved in sharing the Gospel with many children across the world through various camps and vacation Bible schools for children. They have participated in drama and music, taught Bible stories, and spent one-on-one time mentoring in America and overseas. In these different countries and cultural settings, just like when Jesus was here in one human body, there is never a lack of opportunities for showing young children love.

Children across cultures seem to especially crave Physical Touch™, Quality Time™, and Words of Affirmation™ like sponges as nourishment for their souls. Sadly, there seems to be a deficit in our children's lives in these areas, regardless of the financial status or type of home.

It is known that all children prosper when receiving expressions of all the five Love Languages™, but it is a challenge for the one or two main adults in their life to express love in every way daily amid all their other responsibilities. In the old days, they would say, "It takes a village to raise a child." It is true that having aunts, uncles, and grandparents around can fill in some gaps we parents don't take time for. Studying your child's two main Love Languages™ will help you love them more effectively.

What Can I Do?

As parents, we naturally need to think about our children's physical needs such as food, clothes, and schedules, and sometimes we forget the hurts, stresses, or fears that might need attention inside our child's soul. A parent might spend all their energy being with their child, hugging them, serving them, and buying them gifts but never verbally affirming them. If a child especially desires Words of Affirmation™, they may feel unloved even while the parent has done so much to try to show love.

A child who prefers Acts of Service™ may come running inside on a mission to get something quickly. If you intercept them with a hug at that moment, they may find it to be an irritation distracting from their mission. An hour later, they may be sitting down watching something and ask you if you can get them a drink or a snack. Perhaps you roll your eyes. *I am working, and you sit on the couch asking me to get you a drink?* Rightly so, they need to learn to serve and be thoughtful too.

I did learn, though, that surprising a few of my children with a prepared snack and drink on a tray when they were watching a movie made them feel more cared for than spending time listening to them, affirming them verbally, or hugging them. (And it's our secret, but this is how you get your children to enjoy crunching on raw purple cabbage as a snack and teach boys to appreciate sipping hot tea out of dainty cups tucked in between a sweet and a salty snack.)

Still, most of us can never overstay the amount of time our children would enjoy having us just "be" with them. It is, by far, the most excellent earthly investment we will ever make. Learning your child's Love Language™ will ultimately lighten your load by giving you tools to love well in the precious minutes you have with your children.

The goal in learning a child's primary Love Language™ is not to cut out the other ways to show them love but to remember that certain ways mean more to them, meet a need faster, and communicate love more clearly to them. Most children are unaware that they are acting frustrated, disobedient, rebellious, or angry as a result of not feeling genuinely loved.

Children will seek belonging elsewhere if they do not find it in the home. For example, they may seek out individual attention from teachers or other caretakers, becoming clingy and possessive. As hard as the answers may be to hear, I believe we are wise to ask our children's teachers and caretakers about their behavior and responses when we are not in the room.

One way to make your job easier as a parent or mentor is to ask yourself, what can I do for my child today that would express my love? Instead of trying to spend more time, try being very pointed in meeting their needs. This will not only make your attempts more effective and fruitful, but it can also help avoid a grumpy child trying to force you to fill their love tank by clinging or throwing a tantrum while you are trying to take care of your adult responsibilities.

Knowing your children's Love Language™ will make it feel like you are more loving to them, even though you had the same love before. Showing your love in ways that mean more to them allows you to hit the bull's-eye more often in caring for them.

Before the Date

Here are a few homework questions that will hopefully give you some insight into your child's Love Language™. They might just confirm your answers when you discuss the questions on your date.

- What does your child tend to seek from their parent when they arrive home?

  ____

- Does your child pursue Physical Touch™ or want you to verbally affirm them in something they have made or done that day?

  ____

- Is there some activity or action that your child asks for repeatedly when you are busy that irritates you and is very inconvenient?

  ____

- What do they always seem to want others around them to be involved with?

  ____

- How does your child tend to show their affection to you and other loved ones?

  ____

- What seems to hurt your child the most?

  ____

These are all signs showing how your child will actually feel more loved by others. Usually the opposite of what hurts them, done in a positive way, is their primary Love Language™.

Practical Applications

Ways to Speak Children's Love Languages:

- Words Of Affirmation™: Compliment them, give cards and read the words to them, compliment them in front of others for their efforts, tell them how you love them
- Physical Touch™: Cuddle with a story, pat them on the back, hold hands, rub lotion on their feet, do manicures and pedicures, hugs and kisses, comb their hair or scratch their back
- Quality Time™: Give undivided attention, play a game, go on a date, ask about their day, eat together, do chores together, make a craft, watch funny home videos together, tell bedtime stories
- Acts of Service™: Make them meals, help them with chores, help organize their room, tuck them in at night
- Receiving Gifts™: Create little surprises on ordinary days, make a treasure hunt, serve a snack, make birthdays extra special, put favorite treats in their lunchbox, mail a package, bring home a surprise, give a pretty flower

Personal Reflections

Date Questions

Potential Love Languages™ are noted in parenthesis, there is no need to read them to your child along with the question.

1. What do we do at home that makes you feel happy?

    Have you ever lay in the grass and tried to see people or animals in the clouds?

2. Would you rather have me sit beside you and read a book (Quality Time™) or hold you and play with your hair or scratch your back (Physical Touch™)?

3. Do you like it best when I get down and play with you (Quality Time™) or rock you and stroke your hair (Physical Touch™)?

4. Would you rather go shopping with me (Quality Time™) or stay home with a sitter and have me bring you a surprise treat (Receiving Gifts™) when I come back?

5. Would you rather have me tell everyone at supper how well you did your jobs that day (Words of Affirmation™) or just give you a reward secretly after supper (Receiving Gifts™)?

6. Would you rather have me sit on your bed and listen to you or have me come and bring you a drink while you are playing (Acts of Service™)?

7. What do you like to do with me when I am home and not too busy?

    Have you ever been to a zoo, farm, or aquarium? What was your favorite creature?

8. What do you like to do with Grandma and Grandpa?

9. Do you like it best when Grandma sends you a birthday card (Receiving Gifts™) or comes to hug and hold you (Physical Touch™)?

10. Would you rather have me take time to sit and see what you are playing or making (Quality Time™) or have me surprise you with a plate of snacks while you are playing (Acts of Service™)?

What would you buy if you had ten dollars?

Closing question:

Now, is there anything you want to ask me?

Spoken Blessing

Explain that all your children are different and you need God's wisdom to be good parents. Ask the child if they would be so kind and would be willing to pray for you and your spouse so that you can be a good mommy or daddy to your children.

Schedule

Take time to look at your next month's schedule, discuss with your child the next possible date, and pencil it in the index calendar as well as your planner or phone calendar.

Responses to Remember

The Gospel for a Child

My Story

Back in the simple days before I cared about nutrition, my favorite childhood breakfast consisted of pouring Cheerios and raw farm milk over a tall square of homemade frosted chocolate cake. If they were in season, we'd often top those three textures with sliced strawberries or peaches. Sadly, but laughingly, I say that my children have no desire to try these four in a bowl together.

In my childhood home, a casual cereal breakfast like this meant it was our Sunday morning at home between the biweekly Amish church services in our local district. Now, if it was a church service morning, we'd rise earlier to get dressed and gather the family for the traditional breakfast of coffee soup before carefully squeezing together in the back bench of the buggy. My sisters and I sat smoothing out our starched white aprons as our horse's clip-clops joined all the others already on the road at 8:00 a.m.

The Old Order Amish Church Affiliation is made up of hundreds of households and spread out in at least a hundred-mile radius in Ohio. The districts are then divided geographically into group sizes that fit in a church member's house, shop, or barn for the biweekly church services.

Since there is no neutral meeting house, each household takes turns hosting the service presented in a combination of High German and Pennsylvania Dutch languages at their house once a year.

After sitting on the backless benches for the three-hour service, we'd stand around tables where the hosts then served the traditional lunch of deli sandwich and relish items ending with homemade pies and cookies, baked by the neighboring church ladies to assist the hosts. The historical Anabaptist reason for the biweekly services was intended for the families to either rest and pay house visits to each other on the in-between Sunday or to go visit another district of Amish church service in the morning, held at a friend's or relative's home.

If we did stay home on the in-between Sunday, we were encouraged to take time to read something in Uncle Arthur's Bible Story Books set in the forenoon. This children's illustrated hardcover set of condensed and rephrased Bible stories from Genesis through Revelations by Arthur Stanley Maxwell was my exposure to the Creation and Jesus, until some cousin of mine submitted my name to the Mailbox Club program for children.

Somewhere in grade school, I remember walking out to the mailbox excitedly anticipating the next issue arriving in my own name. Reading and filling out the question blanks of these illustrated stories in English helped me apply God's word to practical daily living. All the Scriptures that I had heard at church as a child were read in my third language, which was High German. I was learning the grammatical rules and sounds of the German alphabet but did not yet understand the meanings of some of the words I could read. As we got older, during that in-between Sunday we practiced our German alphabet so we could someday read for ourselves out of the German Bible in our home.

Your Story

How did you view God and the Holy Spirit and Jesus in your childhood? What was your worldview, and who were you in it? Did you consider yourself a sinner in need of a Savior? I didn't until my tween years.

Wouldn't the preschool learning stage be such a good time to build our mentality of God's plan for Creation and why we are even born? A young child may form some fears and anxiety during these first years depending on their exposure to evil and trauma. For them to know about Jesus's gift of sacrifice for their soul in eternity will shape their pattern of thinking as they process the hard and good coming their way in life.

Personal Reflections

On This Date

You will be asking some very basic theological questions to your child to open up a conversation. You can see what they know and what more they would like to know. Take courage that if you have not been exposed to the content of God's Word, preserved through the centuries, you can learn with your children.

Date Questions

See the Gospel Answer Key in the Index for answers.

1. How did this world and all the plants and animals start?

2. Who made everything we can see? Who made you and me?

3. What does the Bible say were the names of the first man and woman?

4. Was God pleased with what He made?

5. What did God say the two people can have to eat?

6. What should they not eat?

7. What would happen if they did eat that?

8. Who came to ask questions to the first woman?

9. What did the woman do after she had discussed what God had said with the snake?

10. What are some other words for not obeying God?

- What is something you remember that you heard someone say in church or children's Sunday school?

- Where is your belly button?

- Do you know the story in the Bible of the flood, and who built a large boat called an ark?

- What is the big night light called that God put up in the sky for us when it's dark?

- What is the big bright thing in the sky called that brings light to the sky in the morning?

Closing question:

Now, is there anything you want to ask me?

Child's Closing Prayer

Parent, have the child repeat one phrase at a time after you.

Dear God, thank you for creating me in my mother's womb. Thank you for knowing my name and where I live. Thank you that you see when I am sad, scared, and happy. Thank you for giving me a healthy body that can walk and play. Thank you that Jesus came as a baby to earth to show us how much you love us. Thank you that Jesus was willing to be hurt on the cross for all the people in the world's bad sins. Thank you for loving me. In Jesus's name, Amen.

Schedule

Take time to look at your next month's schedule, discuss with your child the next possible date, and pencil it in the index calendar as well as your planner or phone calendar.

Responses to Remember

Date 8:

Hints of Their Life Calling

If your child has never heard about Jesus dying for them and the great commission given in Matthew 28:16–20, you may want to go back and do the Gospel for your Child date before this one.

Our Story

One Sunday morning in August, my feet hit the floor early, knowing it was a full day for me and my four little ones. Our lives were being mostly boxed up to relocate to North Carolina, where my husband, Dave, could better carry out his new job as Field Representative for Gospel Express Ministries. In the middle of the packing, Dave had left for a two-week trip to Ghana, Africa, and I was taking our four children, all aged five and under, to church by myself.

After getting all of us ready and eating a light breakfast, we actually arrived early for Sunday school. My carefully prearranged plan proceeded to carefully unravel from there. The four-year-old began whimpering about an earache, so we only dropped off the three- and five-year-olds to their Sunday school classes. My four-year-old joined her one-year-old brother as my squirmy dates to the ladies' class.

Once I, the mother, was all settled in and listening to the lesson, the same ear-aching preschooler began crying to go home. She clutched her lower abdomen in pain. Her stomach felt hard to the touch. All of this should have been alarming, but I became suspicious. This was the same child who could not relax to go into the long oval commodes of a public restroom during an entire summer's day at the zoo, while sipping drinks hour after hour, and held it until we got home at night.

Guessing we were experiencing a repeat, I attempted the church bathroom to alleviate her but to no avail. She clung to me from her perch, acting as if she was in sharp pain. I carried her out past all the Sunday school classes, put her in our vehicle, and drove it up to the carport. Then came the job of extracting our sons from their classes. The three-year-old came willingly while a friend held my baby, but my five-year-old was very disappointed and refused to obey. After finally realizing I would need to leave whether he joins or not, he sulked and stomped out of class. I had just buckled all the siblings into their car seats when I realized the four-year-old had in fact emptied her full bladder into the middle captain seat of our van. Magically, she was now "all better!"

On this same afternoon, I was planning to take my parents, aunt, and uncle to visit my oldest aunt after surgery. Between getting home, making sure everyone had dry clothes and lunch to eat, and running us all to pick up the sitter with no driver's license, I was determined to keep up my mother's tradition and assemble a fresh bouquet from the backyard for my recovering aunt. I buckled in my three-year-old to join our hospital trip as I thought that poor babysitter can only manage so much. Then, the bouquet, which I had so tediously attempted to stabilize, dumped right onto the same seat my four-year-old had emptied her bladder into earlier that morning. "And we know that for those who love God all things work together for good" (Rom. 8:28, ESV). The upside, I decided, was that I could now explain the plastic and towel my passengers perched on. God does have a sense of humor.

What Can I Do?

This is only half of the stress I encountered that day, which, according to my journal, had me breaking out in full hives by Monday. It is days like this that I pray and confess, *Lord, help me to treat my children as you would if you would care for them for a day. Help me to look into their little faces and see the character and person you are molding for your purposes.*

I am aghast, cringing, feeling sorry for us, and laughing all at the same time as I read through some of these rare journal entries from the busy, early years of having our first three children, each sixteen months apart from the next. Our fourth child was added two years later, so at times Dave and I were both seen with one child on each hip. You might say they kept our parenting well balanced. At this stage, I wondered if we could raise these preschoolers to be even mildly well-functioning adults.

These first five years of a child's life are the most thankless and physically wearing. You *can* someday feel caught up with your sleep. You *can* someday experience them coming to you with gratefulness, thoughtfulness, and apologies without being prompted. You *can* someday rejoice in their goals and skill sets as they become an asset to your home instead of a liability.

Although this subject of their life calling seems pretty hazy while in the middle of this all-encompassing servanthood stage, I want to place in your parental vision a mindset that propelled me during that reliant diapers-and-questions stage of our children. Visualizing my child as a person, who will someday be a successful adult influencing many lives, motivated me to treat them with honor. When your child is whining, resisting, or getting loud, stoop down and look into their faces. Remember that this child is a whole person made in the image of God. Do not grow weary in remaining gentle as you teach and train these individuals.

Keep the mindset of Jesus's words in Luke 12:3, that what was spoken in dark will be heard in the daylight and what you have whispered behind closed doors will be proclaimed on the rooftops.

My version of motivation in the fear of God would go something like this: How will my children remember me as a parent? How will they tell their story, and how will the home culture we have established affected them and others?

I give you much room to fail, as I did. Be humble. Apologize and validate what your actions may have done to them. I am here to testify that though your soul despairs somedays like mine did, God does work mightily to redeem things in our children in spite of us and our inconsistencies if we humbly ask Him!

Now seeing the unique, kind, skilled, and beautiful influential adults our little ones have grown into, my husband and I know it was in spite of us, not because of us, that they are who they are today. Were we always consistent? No. Were we always wise, gentle, and kind in our corrections? No. Did we apologize often? Yes. We see that it was more through our faith and prayers for them, and God's huge intervention and favor, that they have become who they are. We realize each of their stories is not finished as even our own are not.

In my journaling of those early years, it is sweet and intriguing to analyze what I said about them as babies and preschoolers. Some of their childhood tendencies are observed to be the same, but thankfully, the negative characteristics that had to do with how they viewed themselves have flipped and faded as both they and we have matured. Dave and I needed to think in faith, train ourselves to speak life and affirmation over our children, and attempt to parent with a more unconditional love.

What vision do you have in faith for your children? On this date, hear what dreams your child has and pray about them in their simplicity. You are an adult with experience and can "pray with understanding" into something they mention as the apostle Paul taught us in I Corinthians 14:15.

Personal Reflections

Date Questions

1. What is something you might want to do when you grow up?
2. What book makes you feel happy, and what book or story makes you feel sad?
3. Who would you like to be like when you grow up?
4. Do you know anyone who you think is lonely or needs a home?
5. How do you like to help people?
6. What is something kind you did for somebody?
7. What makes you sad?
8. Do you ever get angry about how somebody treated someone else?
9. Would you rather go on a trip or stay home?
10. Have you noticed a boy or girl that is very different from you?

- Have you ever seen a rainbow?
- Do you know what colors are in the rainbow? (full scientific answer: red, orange, yellow, green, blue, violet, indigo)
- Do you know which man in the Bible saw the very first rainbow?
- What promise from God do we remember when we see the rainbow in the sky?

Closing question:

Now, is there anything you want to ask me?

Spoken Blessing

Dear Father, you have made this child for a purpose, and I thank you that you have called and trusted me to raise, train, love, and prepare _____________ (their name) for all that you have called (him or her) to be and do. Help me to show (their name) _____________ who you are by how I live and treat (him or her). Please protect this child from anything that wants to come against your plan for this life and empower this child to overcome evil, temptations, and darkness that might try to deter from your purposes. I pray you, God, would put kindness and mercy in their heart toward other children. I pray you will help them to honor and respect all their teachers and authorities in their life so that You can prosper them.

Schedule

Take time to look at your next month's schedule, discuss with your child the next possible date, and pencil it in the index calendar as well as your planner or phone calendar.

Responses to Remember

Date 9:
Recognizing Lies

My Story

It was another crisp Sunday morning as the usher seated me and my four young ones in the third pew from the back. My husband had mission board duties that morning, which would keep him from joining us. My three oldest filed in and sat down, and I followed, settling the baby on my lap.

As the service began, our three-, four-, and five-year-olds were having an intense whispering disagreement. I tried to speak softly and get their attention to no avail. They were not looking my way or hearing my whispers at all. I became very aware of the eyes and ears of the people seated on the benches behind us and tried repeating the name of our oldest son, who was seated in the

middle of his two younger siblings. I realized he couldn't hear me and in quick desperation reached over to pinch his leg.

Reeling in surprise, our firstborn turned toward the

source of sudden leg pain with an innocent, surprised look. His big eyes seemed to ask me, *"Mom, why would you hurt me like that without an explanation?"* Immediately, I regretted my decision. After whispering an apology, I helped them settle their argument but was left unsettled by my parenting tactics. Did I need to intervene? Probably. Was I parenting out of love and concern for my children or a desire to maintain my own reputation? I could see my response was not motivated by a desire to disciple my son but from an immediate reaction to the fear of man.

What Can I Do?

How soon we forget after our baby dedications that our children are the Lord's and we are stewards to raise them! They are not for us. Not even for our comfort and well-being when we are older. It is a blessing if they are there for us, but it is not our right to claim. They are made by and for Him, and He entrusts us to be their caretakers and teachers.

The Holy Spirit revealed what was in my heart that day in the pew. I saw that I had not been acting for the sake of my children, instead acting selfishly because I wanted people's affirmation. I had feared more what our friends in the benches behind me thought of us than how I treated my own children.

God showed me at that moment that I was "provoking my son to wrath" by not loving him as I taught. Ephesians 6:4 warns us not to "provoke our children to wrath" (KJV). God spoke to me gently about rebellion in children stemming from moments as simple as this. I realized I needed humility. I needed to learn to have my children's well-being at heart above my reputation. If not, my children will feel it, and we will reap back from them the dishonor we sowed. Children can read and sense fear, anger, hypocrisy, and impure motives before they can read a written language.

The Kingdom of God is all about discerning motives. God reminded me that perfect love casts out fear, and He faithfully and gently shows me when I am not operating in agape love.

Personal Reflections

Before the Date

The question to ask is not just "How do I parent?" but "What heart motive am I parenting out of?"

The focus of this date is to see if there have been moments in your child's life that affect how they view themselves and relate to others. Whether the hurt or offense came through you or someone else, prepare to listen without disagreement or defense. Aim to show Jesus's compassion and care for their little heart. How your child perceived a scenario may be very different from how you did, but it may still seem true and real to them. Instead of trying to correct them, you can just say sincerely, "I am so sorry for how that felt. Can you forgive them (or me)?"

Date Questions

🌀 Have you ever been on a merry-go-round of horses?

1. What has happened to you that made you feel sad?

2. Have you ever felt very angry about something someone has done?

3. Do you remember any time that I hurt your feelings?

4. Have you ever felt embarrassed by something that someone did?

🌀 Would you rather go fishing or camping?

5. Is there anyone who wants to talk or play with you but you don't feel comfortable with them?

6. Do you think God made you smart and wise?

7. Do you like the way God made your body and how you look on the outside?

8. Do you ever wonder why God made you that way?

9. Did you ever feel like someone didn't like you?

🌀 What animals do you think run the fastest?

10. What is something you would want to learn to do better than you can right now? Why?

🌀 What is your favorite zoo animal?

Closing question:

Now, is there anything you want to ask me?

Prayer About Grievances and Dedication

God and Father, thank you for giving this child ____________ to us.

You have created (him or her) in the way that pleased you, and we like __________ the way you made (him or her).

We give to you the way that ________ has felt ________ (negative emotion) when __________.

Help __________ not to compare (herself or himself) with others but know that (he or she) is good at _____ and ____ and does not need to worry about the rest. We dedicate __________ and (his or her) life and body to you, God, to protect all the days of (his or her) life!

Schedule

Take time to look at your next month's schedule, discuss with your child the next possible date, and pencil it in the index calendar as well as your planner or phone calendar.

Responses to Remember

The Birds and the Bees

Our Story

A young mom explained to her daughter that girls are different from boys because they have a uterus and ovaries in order to have babies someday. She came out of her master bathroom to the scene of her preschool daughter happily jumping up and down on the bed, singing, "I . . . have . . . over . . . ies! I . . . have . . . over . . . ies!"

When we start answering our young children's questions on how God created humans male and female, and all the other questions that go along with that, we show them it is a healthy and safe subject to discuss with us. We want to be the ones introducing and establishing the appropriate terminology and perspective for our children's personal view of their sexuality. At some point, your children will be exposed to opposing beliefs, views, or less desirable terminology of this subject.

When an innocent child has questions and doesn't get them answered by us, the dark agents of this world will use books, movies, games, or other people, including children, to answer those questions in a way that will tarnish their sweet minds. No matter how disqualified you may feel as parents to have this conversation, especially if your parents never did, you are playing offense by talking about it openly.

This is a conversation that can stay open all through their childhood as they encounter new questions or hear new terms about the body. The goal is to never portray as shameful or dirty what God said was good. Evil's agenda is to steal the beauty and preciousness of God's ordained plan. It attempts to portray the consummation of marriage and replenishing the earth as sinful and perverted, or it tries to deceive us to just avoid talking about it entirely. By speaking about sexuality openly, you are setting Kingdom-worthy goals originating from the kingdom of Light's perspective for your child.

What Can I Do?

A few practical ways you can play offense is to have an open-door policy when your children are playing with any other children. This may be at your house, someone else's house, or in a public building. We learned that even in innocent preschool play, such as playing doctor or pretending to breastfeed, children may partly undress or show body parts to each other. Usually they will think twice before doing anything that feels private when the door is open and people could walk by at any time. We explained this rule is for their safety to make sure no one is hurting them or doing something they shouldn't do.

We discourage overnight stays unless you know and trust the hosts very well and can have them checking up on the children's playtime. I tried to make it a habit to ask my children about their times at babysitters' or friends' houses and watched for any signs of discomfort, fear, or guilt as they talked about their time there.

You never want to plant fear or suspicion in your child's heart about someone, but there are a few ways to fish for any suspicious activities. Try asking your child if they want to go again soon. Ask if they feel safe and loved there or if they were scared at any time while at their friend's house. You could ask if they have anything they want to tell you about that might bother them. Abuse victims are usually threatened to never tell anyone, so watch the initial responses in their face and eyes before they have time to put up their guards.

Creating safeguards and healthy boundaries is a proactive step in the prevention of trauma. Asking good questions after children have been away from us and staying aware of what has been happening to them is the second step. We should be wise, but we do not need to parent out of fear. We can only do so much, and then we need to live in trust and faith, instead of inviting evil by verbally continuing to speak out fears. God is redemptive and the Healer for our own childhood circumstances. He can be trusted for the next generation's wholeness as well.

Before the Date

You may want to take time to glance over the spoken blessing offered after the date questions and pencil in the blanks with specific things for your child. Having them done ahead will help you to speak it more smoothly and be more prepared when your child is present. Enjoy having the privilege to be that safe place in your child's life for them to learn or talk about sacred and special things, rather than the world educating the child in its view and terms. You could greatly alter their future and protect them from pain and distrust by talking openly about these things.

Date Questions

1. Did you know at one point when you were in Mommy's tummy, you were small enough to fit in my hand?

2. Did you know that God chose the color of your hair and eyes and skin? And that He knew how you would look before we even got to see you?

3. Do you know the day you were born and came out of Mommy's belly is the same day we celebrate your birthday every year?

4. Have you seen baby animals drink their mommy's milk?

5. Are you glad that God made you a (boy or girl)?

6. What do you like about being a (boy or girl)?

7. Only the people that help you have a bath and get dressed should see you naked. Has anyone else ever looked at your private parts or tried to touch you there?

8. God made your private parts, and they are good, but we cover our bodies so other people don't see our private parts.

9. We should not ask to see anyone else's body parts, that is how we respect their privacy. Have you ever not respected their privacy?

10. Parent: If your child knows someone that is pregnant, ask them if they know that person has a baby growing in their tummy.

🍦 Which is your favorite shirt?

🍦 What is your favorite flavor of ice cream?

Closing question:

Now, is there anything you want to ask me?

Spoken Blessing

I am glad God made you (boy or girl), and I pray someday you will be a good (mommy or daddy) to your children! Thank you, Lord, that you gave ______ (name of child) ______ (color of hair) hair and ________ (color of eyes) eyes and put (him or her) in our family.

Schedule

Congratulations! If you took the dates in order, you have now completed all the subjects we offer for this age level! If you have not completed all the earlier dates for this age level, you can continue having them in the order and pace you prefer.

Responses to Remember

ELEMENTARY

AGES 6–10

POSITION OF ADULT ROLE:

Continuing to activate your growing child's conscience on right from wrong, establishing in their minds what you as parents consider acceptable behavior, speech, and viewing habits, and how you spend time, money, and energy in your established home.

Date 1:

Creating a Safe Culture

My Story

During a weekday outing at a park, I watched a mother reprimand her son for his clumsy actions, humiliating the young boy in front of his friends and their mothers. My heart yearned to comfort the boy as I realized how disrespected he must have felt. Thankfully, my growing judgment for the mother was cut short as God reminded me of my own moments of fear-based mothering.

How often have I scolded or corrected my children in front of people to help me look better among peer parents? When our children showed a lack of character in front of our friends, I knew my focus could, and sometimes did, turn from discipleship of their hearts to self-preservation of my own image. I still want to cry when I think of how this immature and damaging kind of correction grieves our Heavenly Father. This self-serving correction can cause young children to view God in a manipulative light as well, often leading to distrust and identity struggles in our innocent children.

Just like each spouse's identity contributes to the health of a marriage, so a parent's view of themself affects the way they respond to their children. How we relate to our children has everything to do with the value we place on our own lives as well and our children's lives . I think it takes every last day of our Christian journey here on earth to grasp even half of our worth because of Jesus's high payment for us. We are personally known and loved unconditionally by our Creator. My life's goal for myself and others I know is to gain an awareness of who we are aside from anything we do so that we can become whole and free from the fear and pain accumulated as a result of relating with pain-filled people in an unholy world.

What Can I Do?

We want to remember to treat our children with respect to the best of our graces. If I treat my children in a disrespectful and hurtful way so that I am thought well of among my friends, how do I expect to reap honorable, humble, selfless adult children as a result?

Many grown children have a hard time believing and trusting that God our Father has an unconditional, pure, nonperformance-based love for them because of what they have or have not experienced from their parents.

In Matthew 18:6 we read, "Whoever causes one of these little ones who believe in Me to sin, it would be better for him if a millstone were hung around his neck, and he were drowned in the depth of the sea" (NKJV).

Really? Ouch. There is a reference section in the index called "Provoking a Child" that expounds on some ways we as adults might discourage or cause a stumbling block to our children unawares.

So, how can I be a safe parent and still correct and teach my children when we are in the company of others? A wise, applicable gauge is to only discipline young children for direct disobedience, not for a poor *performance* of attempted obedience. Focus on the Family offers a very good article explaining this called "The Discipline Check-up" by Dr. Walt Larimore on their website.

We have found some solutions for public misbehavior in God's Word and have steps on how that looks practically with different-aged children in the index called "Correction in Public."

Creating Your Home Culture

Children learn what is acceptable behavior best in the safety of your home. You can kindly and firmly create your own culture on what is acceptable and what is not. Watch for lighthearted, teachable moments throughout the regular moments in your day, whether they come at meal times, working side by side, relaxing together, or driving down the road. Some weeks, upon noticing certain attributes lacking in our own family, I would pencil in my planner what character training I wanted to focus on cultivating in our home. I preferred to go on the offensive, bringing the subjects up casually, in a positive atmosphere, instead of constantly correcting, fixing, and maintaining our culture defensively.

I learned from watching my husband that it is usually better to address issues in group settings later and to let the incident go at the moment of violation. Once we as parents are calm and have thought and prayed about how to address it, private conversation brings forth much better results.

On This Date

As we open up this series of dates to intentionally listen to your child, it is essential to establish a safe culture. How comfortable is your child opening their heart up in your presence? How equipped is he or she in communicating what's in their heart to you? If your child is not opening up freely to you, ask if their feelings have been hurt or shut down by something you or some other authority have said or done.

As they share from their little person point of view, you may remember what all was not going your way and the pressures or workload you had at the time. It may feel like their hurt or disappointment was minor compared to what all you were experiencing or that their feelings are unfair to your own.

Pride will coach you to offer excuses if your child brings something to you, but now is the time to recognize remorse. If we want to be a safe place, we will need to learn to put others first by listening without arguing or defending ourselves.

An offender's unawareness, pressures of the circumstance, pure motives, or the accidental nature of the occurrence is not something to bring up now. After the date you can take time to get to the index for your own "Heart Care" about the circumstance they are discussing, if it helps you move past it and be at peace yourself. You may clarify that how they took it is not how you meant it. You can both acknowledge how the child felt and how they were saddened and tell them how you genuinely view them with love and affection.

It is not a child's job to comfort you in your uncontrollable circumstance or shoulder blame for what you are going through. Even if your child provoked you to anger, you are the more mature one and are responsible for your own responses. I realize when they speak their negative emotions, you want to tell them how you felt in that same circumstance. There is a Heart Care section in the index for you to take time by yourself before

God to process what may have triggered your hurtful response in that same circumstance. You matter as well.

On the child's part, don't be too hard on yourself if at first they seem reserved. This process of building trust is best explored gently over time, and you can use these series of dates to build a fresh culture of safety between you and your child.

I hope on this date:

1. You will try to remember that any words and actions that hurt a person will feel painful whether or not the offending party meant harm.
2. If the child shares that you hurt them, you can repeat back to them how you heard it made them feel.
3. You can ask about how it affected them and maybe still is affecting them.
4. Make yourself vulnerable and soft and by apologizing humbly if needed for any intended or unintended harm, even if your motive was pure.

Date Questions

 What is one of your favorite memories that we have done together as a family?

1. Did either of us parents ever promise you something that we never followed through with?

2. Have tried to forgive me for any words I've said but you keep thinking about them?

3. Do you remember something us parents did that embarrassed you?

If you won two round-trip plane tickets to anywhere, where would you go, and who would you take with you?

4. Do you have a memory of a circumstance where I hurt your feelings or you felt angry because of something I said or did? Ephesians 6:4

5. Have I done something that makes it harder for you to trust me?

6. Who is the easiest person to talk to in our family?

7. Does it feel like one person is more praised or appreciated than another at home?

8. Who in your life is your most trusted and safe person to be with?

9. What is something that I could do that would really encourage you?

Who is someone in history you would want to be like?

10. Do you have any questions you would like to ask me?

Who is someone famous you would love to meet?

Testimony Video

Spoken Blessing

Face your child and maintain eye contact.

(Name of child)________________, I really enjoy how you ______________ and appreciate your willingness to ________________. You always seem willing and ready to ________________ if I have time. I en-joy ________________ with you. Our home is a better place because of how you try to make ______________ a priority and work as team with ______________ to ______________. I want us both to feel safe to share anything with each other without feeling judged or offended.

Schedule

Take time to look at your next month's schedule, discuss with your child the next possible date, and pencil it in the index calendar as well as your planner or phone calendar.

Responses to Remember

Date 2:
Routines and Relationships

Our Story

Can any of you relate to grimacing from the kitchen as several sons grunt and thump to the ground in a tackling match? Or perhaps a combative game of balloon volleyball, sponge softball, or mini hoops basketball sends small objects whizzing past your head. If you have two or more boys, you may feel a kinship with me.

During our first years in the Carolinas, we homeschooled in a tiny storage room, endured much "gym activity" in our formal living room, and got accustomed to reading bedtime stories cross-legged on the carpet between the four children bunking in one bedroom. I was delighted and refreshed when my husband designed and added two spacious rooms to our bulging academy.

We have home videos of the many beautiful hours of memories our children made under the vaulted ceiling of the schoolroom, which doubled as a carpeted gym, and in the large boys' bedroom that expanded opportunities for activity during the scorching heat of summer and few freezing winter months in the south.

Among that recorded footage is a scene of our youngest five-year-old son, pinned down by the weight of his heftier brother, calling out innocently, "Angels come!" We laugh as we remember how I had come up with a rule that they may wrestle as long as neither one of them is angry, crying, or calling for mercy. Often, you would hear them grunting, rolling, panting, and squealing. When someone yelped in pain, the other would whisper, "Shhh, don't cry, you know we'll have to stop if Mom hears you." It comforted me to know that if the smaller child actually needed help, all they had to do was ask.

A few years later, our oldest son was maturing and moved out of that physical combat stage, and I noticed the younger boys getting back into more physical rivalry between the two of them. I mentioned my concern to the oldest brother, whom the second son used to play with the most. His reply was, "That's good, Mom. Don't you see the two of them are bonding more with each other now?" *Really?* My oldest son was known for his care and protection of his brothers, so I took his view as advice and tried to comfort myself at the sound of each new groan and grunt. As they got older and larger, these matches were enough to shake the forty-five-foot coach bus we were all cooped up in for travels. Seeing the chances of being slammed into as very probable, I would laughingly call "hide the women and children!" as the rest of us escaped into the back of the bus until one pinned the other on the couch for the final triumph. Whenever we'd hear the forceful testosterone all end in a pile of laughter, we'd reenter the fun zone.

In less jovial episodes, where retaliation and forceful punches of anger are behind the tussle, we as parents may miss the fact that one child may be aggravating the other by the words they are saying. When they were younger, if one child attacked the other and it seemed vengeful, I would halt the combat to investigate. I often asked the one being attacked, "Did you say or do anything that would have invited this aggressive response?" It's my application for our home culture of Ephesians 6:4, "And ye Fathers, provoke not your children to wrath, but bring them up in the nurture and admonition of the Lord" (KJV). I believe this can apply to all people in how we are not to treat any humans, we should never "provoke or tempt each other to the point of anger" for our own advantage. The Golden Rule in Luke 6:31 sums up a good standard for our homes, teaching us to be kind, long-suffering, and to treat others as we want to be treated.

In our home we attempted to respond to tattling, accusing, arguing, and belittling with positive, creative solutions. I will once again bring in Matthew 18:15 for a solid solution for sibling rivalry or approaching someone who has hurt us. I am also amazed what a creative and flawless solution this is for adults when tattling happens. Matthew 18:15 tells us that if anyone sins against you, you should approach them personally about it first. So if one of our children came complaining loudly about one of the others to me, I would try to hush their rant and explain that we will go to that person, and they can tell them exactly what they just told me.

The sweet thing was that the child was usually much kinder telling the sibling or friend what they had done face-to-face than when they were announcing it to me. They usually calmed down and acted civil and talked more like grown-ups, realizing that the other child is aware they probably weren't being an angel themselves. Often both ended up apologizing and making up without me needing to coach them on repentance and apologies, especially once this principle was established and familiar to them.

A few things that happen in this process are:

- The offended child feels validated that they matter because you are stopping your project to go with them to solve the problem.
- Both children become aware that everyone's voice and feelings matter in this home and not just theirs alone.
- I will ask the offender to look at the squealer and ask them to explain what they are upset about and how it made them feel. Watching the squealer soften when face-to-face with the offender continues to remind me of why God put that principle in the instruction manual for human conflict.
- Often the offender realizes how it affected the squealer. If they have been taught proper apology, they will often acknowledge and apologize for their part of the conflict.
- I am always refreshed and awed by how often the squealer will also be convicted of their self-focused mindset and apologize for an earlier offense or attitude. It's modeling healthy human interactions for their grown life.

As far as the accusing, arguing, and belittling, there could be various responses according to the circumstance.

If we were home, we would often ask the one speaking negatively about another family member to speak three positive attributes they see in that other person's life in front of all who are in the room. We all enjoy it and are humored observing the awkward scene. As referees, we don't accept lame flattery or passive-aggressive attempts at encouragement. This is a good way for our children to learn how to communicate speaking words of life as well as pleasantly surprising and honoring the recipient with the good characteristics this sibling observes in them.

If the scenario is not appropriate for that kind of time and activity, we will simply observe. If it seems slightly truthful and therefore hurtful, we remind the speaker that if not everyone is having fun, then no one is and expect an apology from them.

On This Date

On this date try to be sensitive to how your child is viewed and treated at home, school, church, and with friends. How is that shaping this child? What is their response like to the treatment? We can't shield our children from being hurt, but we can help them learn how to respond to them and process them before the Lord.

When our oldest children were between the ages of eight and twelve, we started feeling like their friends had more influence on them than we did. This is no picnic and enough to turn inexperienced parents to new measures of administration through bribing or other sorts of manipulation. This was a wake-up call for my husband and me, and God taught us and our children much in the next years. Our oldest ones shared a very helpful insight with us when our last three came through that stage. They told us:

1. Don't take the rejection or reactions personally when they resist the family standards we had established. Because at that stage of life, a child will ask for anything that will hopefully make them more accepted and liked. In a year or two, when their

bodies have stopped changing and they feel more secure, it will no longer be such a big deal, and they will more likely respect us for knowing what we believe and carrying it out in a gentle, loving way.

2. Our older children reminded us that they have friends and that they need parents. Someone secure and firm and wise to lead and walk them through all the questions.

3. I personally learned to remind myself I am the adult, they need me. Yes, I can be their friend but not a wishy-washy one. If they slam doors or cry or yell, it's because they have hormonal days and moments as do I. They will have better days, or they will come crying into our arms when the world is cruel. We are their safe place.

This is a good stage to pray Malachi 4:6: "And He will turn the hearts of the Fathers to the children, and the hearts of the children to their fathers, lest I come and strike the earth with a curse" (KJV). I remember a season where my husband and I were claiming this verse and humbly asking God to create, deepen, or renew this kind relationship with our children.

I hope you can intentionally receive Malachi 4:6 for your family and enjoy the process as you allow God to turn your hearts toward each other.

Personal Reflections

Date Questions

Offense Check: Is there anything in your heart that I do, have done, or have not done in the past that irritated, belittled, hurt, shamed, angered, or let you down that might hinder you from trusting me and opening up on our date today?

 What is your favorite thing to order at a coffee or ice-cream shop?

1. Who are the easiest people for you to get along with in our family?

2. Is there anyone in your life that thinks or does things very differently from you? Is it hard to understand them?

Which of your teachers is your favorite and why?

3. What stresses you out most in our home?

4. Have you been able to forgive everyone that has misunderstood or hurt you?

If you could enter the Olympics, what sport would you enjoy competing in?

5. Can you think of a time when you dishonored someone with your words or hurt their feelings and never made it right?

6. What are some ways that you try to practice or want to "do unto others as you would have them do to you" as Jesus taught? (Matthew 7:12)

What era in history would seem fun for you to live in and why?

7. Are there any upsetting feelings between you and any of your brothers and sisters that feel like a wall between you?

8. Has anything ever happened between you and your brothers or sisters that bothers you but you haven't felt free to tell anyone?

9. Do you see someone doing hard work or kind, unselfish things for others that you think I should know about?

10. Have you ever thought of an additional rule or reward system we as parents could put in place that would help encourage better management in our home?

 Who was your favorite king, queen, or president, and what did they do?

Closing Question:

Do you have any questions you'd like to ask me?

Spoken Blessing

Lord, Bless _____________ for how (he or she) _________________ and _______________ at home. Bless (him or her) for encouraging his siblings by _______________. Thank you for what (he or she) brings into our home and help (him or her) to respond in a kind and loving manner when _____________ or _______________ don't always treat (him or her) with respect and gentleness. In Jesus's powerful Name, Amen.

Remember, a hug goes a long way.

Schedule

Take time to look at your next month's schedule, discuss with your child the next possible date, and pencil it in the index calendar as well as your planner or phone calendar.

Resource

For practical teaching on what is considered good manners from table to cell phone to introductions in answering the phone or door, Monica Irvine's free etiquette factory videos are a fun and quick way to remind all of us. See her YouTube channel or her website for lots of resources.

https://www.youtube.com/watch?v=Q3GAhPHNjg8
https://theetiquettefactory.com/about.php

Responses to Remember

Maintaining a
Clear Conscience

Our Story

I remember a close friend calling me concerned about a view they had noticed on their computer history, which had been during some screen time our children had during their visit. She didn't know if it was accidental or just curiosity, but wanted to be responsible for our children's time in their home and made us aware of it.

What has been your experience so far with new things your school-age child is being exposed to? It's never fun for any of us parents to get negative information we are unaware of about our children. The disappointing circumstance can trigger our own guilt or shame if we haven't worked through our past.

In hindsight, I would like to encourage you not to dread but rather embrace the thought that you get to be the one who introduces your growing child to discover and navigate through the more mature matters in life. Whether it's planned or untimely, those teachable moments can all turn into memorable, bonding discussions if you carefully take time to make them just that.

I am glad and sad to say that my husband and I have found it a better experience to have preteens and adolescents than the experience we gave our parents when we were that age. One good thing about shameful regrets in our past is that we can be more knowledgeable and relatable with our children walking through these experiences.

Your Own Heart Care

Before you help your child process on this date, is there anything bothering your own conscience? Is there something you need to examine or confess in order to walk in confidence before God?

I John 3:19–22 says, "And by this we know that we are of the truth, and shall assure our hearts before Him. If our heart condemns us, God is greater than our heart. And knows all things. Beloved if our heart does not condemn us, we have confidence toward God. And whatever we ask we receive from Him. Because we keep his commandments and do those things that are pleasing to his sight. And this is His commandment, that we should believe in the name of His Son, Jesus Christ and love one another as He gave us commandment" (ESV).

The first two verses here are for us to examine ourselves. Once we have taken inventory of our conscience, the following two verses give us freedom to come to our Heavenly Father with anything as long as we are walking in His instructions to our best ability. The final one reminds us that Jesus's unconditional love is supposed to be carried out in our relationships with others, pleasant or unpleasant.

This last part of the final verse reminds us of the importance of agape love, which also applies to parenting, even when the children lack in carrying out our expectations as well as Jesus's commandments.

One way to test whether we are exercising agape parenting and to gauge how safe we are as parents is to ask: how do we respond to our children's failures?

What Can I Do?

When our children fail to obey, if we correct and instruct in a loving manner, they can see what a just but gracious, gentle Father we have in Heaven. It is important not to discipline a child who is trying to obey but is unable to carry out a task in the way you would desire.

Demonstrating what is expected or helping with the task to improve performance is called training. We must remember to distinguish this from discipline for lack of obedience. Giving and withholding affirmation or rewards is an excellent way to teach a lesson while training, but we must aspire to avoid demeaning children's self-worth with hurtful words at all times.

When our children fail in integrity, we can ask how we can help in the future. You could suggest monthly accountability with a parent or mentor, create safeguards with their phone, or put boundaries in place around certain friendships. If punishment is the immediate result of honest confessions, you can communicate to your child that it is better for future failures and sins to be kept secret from you.

Remember how your Heavenly Father responds to your confession of sins. Natural consequences are often a result of sinful actions, but mercy flows from God to us in the middle of them when we repent. If you feel some type of consequence is expedient for your child, you can ask God for creativity on what type would be best to still treat them with the honor they may not deserve.

Find a consequence that correlates with the transgression. For example, keeping their phone in the kitchen during certain hours for a time period or writing out and memorizing verses that pertain to victory in the subject at hand. Remember that being treated with honor is likely to increase your child's desire to live honorably.

I hope on this date:

1. You can assist and teach your child how to unpack and lift any burdens from others or any secret sins that may be hindering them from having a clear conscience and fully enjoying life.
2. You can have a friendly tone with a kind face as you approach these questions, and I pray the trust would grow between you two through it.
3. Once they feel free from the guilty conscience, then hopefully they will keep feeling safe to ask you about other difficult things they face in the future , just like our approachable Heavenly Father.
4. If the child confesses inappropriate activity, remember that curiosity is innocent learning and should never be shamed. (See "shaming" section in index.)
5. You use this date as an opportunity to kindly activate their conscience for a lifetime on what is "respectful" and what is not, without making them feel guilty.
6. If today you created a safe, bonding experience for them, it will open the door for them to feel welcome to come to you with their biggest concerns.

If your child confesses something shameful that bothers their conscience, no matter how minuscule or big, remember to smile kindly and show affection and sympathy toward their shame and regret. Be sure to lead them in prayer of confession out loud to clear their conscience of the offense. The next step is to discern whether they, or you and your child, should go to anyone else to make things right, showing them the important process of restitution between people. "Follow peace with all men, and holiness without which, no man shall see the Lord" (Hebrews 12:14, KJV).

Personal Reflections

Date Questions

Offense Check: Is there anything in your heart that I do, have done, or have not done in the past that irritated, belittled, hurt, shamed, angered, or let you down that might hinder you from trusting me and opening up on our date today?

 If someone would pay for a plane ticket for you to go anywhere in the world, where would you want to go, and what is it you would want to do there?

1. Is there anything that bothers you or is stressing you out that you would like to talk to God about?

What's your favorite outdoor and indoor activity and why?

2. Do you have any secrets you'd like to get rid of that hinder your relationship with God or any person?

If you could choose where you could travel to for a week, where would it be?

3. Have you read or heard any new words and don't know what they mean?

4. Has anyone ever asked you to keep something embarrassing, shameful, sinful, or harmful a secret and told you to promise to never tell anyone?

   Parent: Explain that this can be something they, you, or someone else has done. Whether it was done to you, with you, or without you.

What is your favorite way to unwind and relax if you have chill time?

5. Is there anyone you try to avoid and don't like to talk to?

6. Is there someone you think is cute?

7. What has been your experience with your friends on the subjects of smelling glues, vaping, smoking, chewing tobacco, drugs, and alcohol? Have you ever been offered or personally tried smoking or drugs?

8. Parent: Share honestly any of your own experiments, temptations, or experiences.

9. Would you like to dedicate your body to God for His protection and to be used only for His glory since He bought you with His blood?

10. Is there anything else you want to get rid of from your conscience or memory?

11. Do you feel you can trust me, and do you feel protected by me?

 Would you rather jump in a pool of chocolate milk, whipped cream, blueberries, slime, cotton candy, or Skittles?

Closing Question

Do you have any questions you'd like to ask me?

Spoken Blessing

I am here to help free you from this burden by taking it to God in prayer. We as parents want to be the protectors of your heart and walk with you in the hard and happy things you go through in life, if you can trust us and share what's going on.

Thank you for your time and honesty, I've enjoyed our time together. Can we finish up our time together by committing these things to God in prayer?

Lead your child in a prayer of confession: Heavenly Father, thank you that you have watched over me and known me even before I was born. I am grateful that you see the hard times and good times I go through here on earth. You know the times I was tempted and struggled with ______________ and ______________. Please forgive me for giving into the temptation and cleanse me from the guilt and shame by Jesus's precious blood shed for me. Take back the ground I gave over to the enemy by opening that door to evil and replace it with your goodness, purity, faith, peace, and renewed joy. Thank you for your grace to start over! I ask for your power to be an overcomer in future temptations by your grace. In Jesus's powerful Name, Amen.

Schedule

Take time to look at your next month's schedule, discuss with your child the next possible date, and pencil it in the index calendar as well as your planner or phone calendar.

Responses to Remember

Date 4:
The Gospel

My Story

Compared to many children, I experienced a pretty innocent, carefree childhood. Although our home was affected by hard things from my parents' past, they never physically hurt us, and their hearts had always been to protect and provide for us. In this stage of childhood, we are eager to learn and experience, and there is so much opportunity for people to influence us. My mindset, view of God, and understanding of eternity was all influenced by those around me.

I assumed God was why we lived and dressed differently than most people around us, but God Himself wasn't freely talked about in conversations. I would have been more familiar with verses from His Word than applying the faith to experience Him as real in my daily life.

Our home held the Amish tradition of silent prayer at meal times. As we knelt in the living room at bedtime, our father read one prayer out loud from the German Prayer Book written by our Anabaptist forefathers. I never asked why we prayed silently, so I just assumed it was established from Matthew 6:5, "And when you pray, you shall not be like the hypocrites. For they love to pray standing in the synagogues and on the corners of the streets, that they may be seen by men. Assuredly, I say to you, they have their reward in full. But you when you pray, go into your room, and when you have shut your door, pray to your Father who is in the secret place: and your Father who sees in secret will reward you openly" (NKJV).

What Can I Do?

These daily habits of prayer in my childhood were reminders of a Higher Power in our lives, as were the church service sermons and songs. I would read some articles in the monthly mailings written by Christians of like faith, which included stories and parables with spiritual meanings and challenges for our daily living.

A new experience of faith happened when I spent the night at a school friend's house from the New Order Amish Church. I will never forget that her dad talked to God out loud about her little brother's broken leg. I was bewildered that they would believe the God of the universe would know Stephen! And would He really care about Stephen's leg in a cast?

Another impactful moment happened when my family piled together on the worn backseat of a dusty, hired car. The driver played a Gospel preaching on the radio that I had never heard before. It was personal and kind, and I pondered the message for hours after we got home.

I also received Mailbox Club letters explaining the Gospel to children. Why did I never apply the message and pray to God that closing sinner's prayer in each Mailbox Club letter? I did not think we believed in that instant salvation stuff, so I resisted, heeding to what I thought my parents and relatives would consider false teaching.

How sobering. I take full responsibility for my actions and choose to glean this from it: as adults, we have so much influence on children through how we live even more than through what we teach.

I have heard it said that those in the eternal lake of fire will remember each time they heard the Gospel of Jesus while on earth and had an opportunity to respond. I am forever grateful that I did not pass into eternity before nineteen years of age when I finally personally responded to the Spirit's promptings in my life and realized the need for a Savior to personally cleanse me of my sins.

Your Story

How did you look at God when you were 6–10 years old? Did you have enough faith to talk to a High Being? If so, whose life did you watch to gain some faith in their God? How did you look at Jesus? Did you know that there is a Holy Spirit dwelling in people on earth? How? Were you exposed to prayer, worship, and God's written Word? Was it all positive or some negative in the presentation? I ask you these questions so that you can remember and, therefore, relate out of your own experiences to your child. Your story could alter their path of life and eternity.

Personal Reflections

On This Date

1. I hope you can together look for any answers that your child has been wondering about concerning God.
2. I hope that the child can understand you better and maybe relate to you in a deeper way because of hearing your childhood experiences back when your faith was nonexistent or new.
3. I hope you will have a clear understanding of where your child is at in their faith and what might be hindering him or her from trusting their Creator God and understanding their own need for a Savior.

Date Questions

Offense Check: Is there anything in your heart that I do, have done, or have not done in the past that irritated, belittled, hurt, shamed, angered, or let you down that might hinder you from trusting me and opening up on our date today?

See the Gospel Answer Key in the Index for answers.

1. Do you consider yourself:

   - A good person since birth,

   - Aware that you have a sinful nature that wants to do things you shouldn't do,

   - Used to be a condemned sinner but repented and received God's gift of Salvation, or

   - Feeling condemned and sometimes hopeless to do right.

2. When or where did sin come on the earth and start in humans?

   - When God made the sun, moon, plants, animals, and Adam.

   - When Adam's wife, Eve, listened to the serpent and disobeyed God.

   - When Jesus was born as a son to Joseph and Mary.

   - When God saw all the wickedness and brought a flood over all the earth.

 If you could travel to space, what would you want to see?

3. Does a baby go to Heaven if it stops breathing and dies?

    - Yes

    - No

    - Only if its parents are Christian believers

4. Why did Jesus leave such a beautiful, perfect place to become a baby and live like a human on earth with unkind and wicked people?

    - To condemn bad people and care for the righteous.

    - To tell us how wrong we are and that we need to stop sinning.

    - To show the Devil how pure Jesus is.

    - To show us who God is and die as a sacrifice for the sins of all people.

    What does the Bible say the rainbow is for us?

5. Do you believe everybody's soul will keep on being somewhere when their body stops breathing?

    - Yes

    - No

    - Only if they were evil on earth

    - Only if they were good on earth

    - Only if they had faith in Jesus as God's Son

6. Have you ever felt God's Presence or thought He said something to you?

7. Have you felt guilty and didn't know what to do about it?

8. If you ever pray, when and how often do you pray? What do you pray about?

9. If someone were to ask you what is your faith or religion, what would you say?

10. If you don't know for sure that you are a Christian believer, do you believe now and desire to become one?

🍦 What are some cuss words that you hear and wonder what they mean?

🍦 Who do you know that you would say has a strong faith and why?

🍦 Is there anything about church that makes you uncomfortable?

🍦 Do you have any ideas that would make church services better for children?

🍦 Who of your friends do you think are probably Christians who live by faith in Jesus?

Closing Question:

Do you have any questions you'd like to ask me?

Repeated Prayer for Child

Have the child repeat after the parent or read out loud.

Dear God and Lord Jesus, Your Word says in Romans 10:9 "that if you confess with our mouth the Lord Jesus and believe in your heart that God has raised Him from the dead, you will be saved." I confess out loud that you are the Christ, the son of God who died and rose again so I can be saved by your shed blood. I ask you to forgive me of all my sin and cleanse me by your shed blood on the cross. I repent and want to be baptized in your Name.

I ask that you write my name in the Book of Life and put Your Spirit inside me so I can be reborn into your Kingdom.

Thank you for dying for me and please finish the work you have begun in me. Thank you for adopting me into your big family. Now I am not my own but bought by you into salvation and eternal life. Help me to know you more and more and become like you. Thank you for this date with _____________ and that you care about me and have called and invited me to You! I believe I am a child of God.

Schedule

Take time to look at your next month's schedule, discuss with your child the next possible date, and pencil it in the index calendar as well as your planner or phone calendar.

Responses to Remember

Love Language

The 5 Love Languages: The Secret to Love that Lasts
by Dr. Gary Chapman

Acts of Service™, Receiving Gifts™, Physical Touch™,
Words of Affirmation™, Quality Time™

Our Story

The soft little fist gently snuggled into my cupped hand and slowly twisted back and forth. From the beginning, our fifth child used to clasp my whole finger with her strong baby grasp while I fed or rocked her. When she started talking and wanted to be held, she would walk up to us, kindly look up, and ask, "Can I hold you?" Even to this day, this child feels loved when we snuggle up beside her or scratch her arm softly.

Whether sitting beside each other during family meeting time or traveling, we all knew two of the siblings were getting their Love Language™ cup filled, whether tussling or giving head scratches or back rubs. Even through high school grammar lessons during homeschool, our daughter would often reach up to cup and twist her hands in mine as we read sentences and laughed through tears at the bad grammar choices. Emotional and mental bonds can also be made through healthy dialogue, whether Quality Time™ or Words of Affirmation™ are on the top of their list of Love Languages™ or not.

This is our experience with one child, but then we have another who bristled at being touched during certain years. He would have much rather had us study and understand him or get him a thoughtful gift than hug him. We encourage parents to continue physically loving those children anyway, whether it's a casual side hug, rubbing their shoulders or feet, or caring for sore muscles, wounds, and scrapes. Children need to get that physical touch from safe people while they are going into puberty and their sexual drive will be heightened. This normally occurs from the age of ten to fifteen.

Caring for Yourself

Two ways to quickly determine what your own Love Language™ might be is to ask yourself these questions:

1. What have been my deepest hurts?
2. In what way could a dad have shown me that he loved me more?
3. In what way would I desire most that my parents, family, spouse, and friends show their love to me?

If you look at the Love Languages™ listed and think you know what yours is, take time to reflect. Tell God any sadness you feel if your family didn't know how to love you well. Maybe seek His Grace to forgive what they didn't know how to give. If you can, pray mercy and blessings on them, thanking God that through the revelation of His love for you, you can then give away what you never experienced from your earthly family.

If you have a spouse, it would be expedient to take time to get to know their Love Language™ so that you can communicate your love in a way that actually connects with them.

Oh, and don't be afraid to tell your child toward the end of the date what your Love Language™ is so they know how to love you better!

Personal Reflections

Caring for Your Child

This date and the questions listed are to confirm what you may already detect to be this child's primary Love Languages™. The key is to document what they are in a visible list, either on a paper or in your phone, so you can remind yourself how to love your child most effectively. Take time to intentionally love your child in their own language daily or at least weekly.

Date Questions

Offense Check: Is there anything in your heart that I do, have done, or have not done in the past that irritated, belittled, hurt, shamed, angered, or let you down that might hinder you from trusting me and opening up on our date today?

1. What is the best way for someone to show you they love and care about you?

2. Is it more meaningful for you to receive a nice gift (Giving Gifts™) or have someone spend time with you (Quality Time™) or give you a hug (Physical Touch™) or compliment you when they greet you? (Words of Affirmation™)

3. Would you rather someone offer to bring you a drink (Acts of Service™ or Giving Gifts™) and snack or just come and be with you? (Quality Time™)

4. Does it mean more to you for someone to watch what you do (Quality Time™) and compliment you on your skills (Words of Affirmation™) or just join you to do it with you? (Quality Time™ or Acts of Service™)

5. Would you choose to go on a trip with someone (Quality Time™) or just have them bring a surprise home for you? (Giving Gifts™)

6. Would it be more of a treat for us to snuggle or give backrubs (Physical Touch™) or just walk and talk? (Quality Time™)

7. What would you want me to do with you if I am home and not too busy?

8. Are you ever glad you are sick or have a wound so that we parents touch and care for you more like we used to when you were little? (Physical Touch™ or Acts of Service™)

9. Would you rather have us read a book together (Quality Time™) or I read something you wrote and compliment you on it? (Words of Affirmation™)

10. Would a hug (Physical Touch™), kind words (Words of Affirmation™), or a surprise ice-cream cone (Giving Gifts™) be more encouraging when you are down?

🍦 What would be one of your favorite activities or ways to spend time together when you are with your friends?

Closing Question

Do you have any questions you'd like to ask me?

Ask Your Child to Pray over You

Ask them if they would pray to the Lord, asking Him to help you as parents to remember each child's Love Language™ and be able to show them love more adequately through their personal Love Language™ even with all your other responsibilities.

Schedule

Take time to look at your next month's schedule, discuss with your child the next possible date, and pencil it in the index calendar as well as your planner or phone calendar.

Date 6:

Recognizing Lies

Our Story

"Are you ready?!" she whispered excitedly to her little brother and mother as they took long, quiet strides toward the closed bedroom door.

Our six-year-old daughter loved to turn every event into a ceremony with special food and an atmosphere conducive to relational connection. She had pulled her four-year-old brother in to help execute her plans. With Mother's supervision, they made a little frosted birthday cake and quickly practiced a catchy birthday rhyme that the sister was coercing her little brother to help sing. She imagined with glittering expectation the moment their newly seven-year-old brother would wake up and come out of his room on his birthday morning. The four-year-old brother didn't want to sing the rhyme, expecting it would sound cheesy and childish to his big brother, now so grown up in first grade.

This four-year-old, much more grounded in reality, saw through his big sister's ideals and envisioned the ordeal would turn awkward fast. Well, that four-year-old was right. The birthday boy emerged sleepily, caught off guard in the spotlight, took in the silly posse at his door singing their birthday rhyme, and responded to it all with a shrug. Glittering little-sister visions crashed to the ground, and little brother's realism might as well have said, "I told you so."

Mother happened to be recording the surprise moment, so every negative emotion passing between the three siblings has been preserved forever in the family vault of childhood DVDs. Our family can watch it over and over if we can bear the pain of the moment. Sometimes we cringe, feeling sorry for all three of them, other times we want to blame the person with the disastrous idea or the birthday boy who hurt his sibling's feelings.

This is an example of a scenario where no one was at fault, yet three innocent people experienced negative emotions. It does not take ill intentions for people to leave a scene with a scar of negativity. Sometimes that negative emotion can create a path of thinking, which leads to a lie that person believes. Sometimes the negative emotion resurfaces whenever that person is put in uncomfortable circumstances that feel similar.

For example, that four-year-old boy could be very triggered when he is asked to do something charitable or kind that his peers may not think is cool. He could become afraid that the recipients of his kindness will disapprove or not want him around because of it. This could create a fear of awkward or childish, girlish ideas, or perhaps he could correlate rejection or discomfort with birthday surprises or morning cheerfulness.

The six-year-old girl could conclude that her ideas are worthless or bad. She could develop a fear of being creative in doing things for others or in surprising people. A fear of rejection or feeling foolish could overshadow her creativity or ability to offer gifts to others.

The birthday boy could possibly feel from then on that his birthday carries obligations to do things other people deem fun and exciting instead of what he actually enjoys. Or he could connect birthday singing or surprises with embarrassment. He might find the spotlight to be awkward and avoid it ever being on him.

Thankfully, I am not aware that these children have scars or identity issues from this particular event, but it only takes little moments like these for us humans to form a lie and believe it. Life happens. Every child on earth will experience moments when they could potentially develop negative patterns of thinking. In the index help section called "Why Am I Triggered?" we demonstrate how adults can help our children process lies they believe about themselves and others through simple thoughtless moments or ignorance, without casting unmerited blame.

Your Relationships

Jesus said offenses will come. So every person in the world will experience rejection and hurt of some kind, no matter what their situation in life. Scripture gives guidance to our response in these moments: "Be angry and sin not" (Eph. 4:26a, KJV), "Vengeance is mine, saith the Lord" (Rom. 12:19), "He opened not his mouth" (Isa. 53:7), "Be ye therefore wise as serpents and harmless as doves" (Matt. 10:16), and "Love your neighbor as yourself" (Mark 12:31).

Let's teach our children how to respond to offenses and not let the enemy gain a foothold through experiences that will inevitably come. One way to play offense and prevent lies from lodging in our children's lives is to be aware daily and weekly. After they leave an event with other people, you can simply ask them, "What was your favorite thing that happened while you were there?" Following up with, "Was there any awkward, hurtful, or not so fun conversations? Was anything uncomfortable?"

If your child gets used to sharing vulnerable feelings with you while they're young, you can much more easily stay connected to their state of being for the rest of their life.

Let's take the "awkward birthday song" happening and I will use it as an example of how I would walk my children through it.

1. I would ask, "Can we sit down and talk about what just happened?"
2. I would ask the thoughtful sister to share why she wanted to do this for her big brother. (Now we all hear her heart's motive and goals.)
3. I would ask the four-year-old how he felt about doing it with her. (We hear his fear and concern going through with it but his desire to honor his big sister.)
4. I ask the birthday boy what went through his mind as he opened the door sleepily into this surprise scene. (We hear how it made him feel awkward with me recording him, the song, and us all looking at him. This helps us understand him not being prepared, so we can forgive him for the negative response that seemed so rude and discouraging.)
5. Each one sees how their actions caused the others to feel uncomfortable, and they realize they had not thought about each other's feelings.
6. To take it to a counseling level of heart care, I would

ask each one to name the negative emotion(s) they felt (see Negative Emotions list in index if needed), and then have them all ask for forgiveness. It is important they learn to show love and mercy to each other without accusing anyone or casting blame. Showing them how to each take responsibility for their own thoughtlessness without defending themselves, honoring the other one over them. (See index subject "Why Am I Triggered?" for more details.)

Personal Reflections

On This Date

You are listening discerningly for any past incidents that may have affected this child that they never told anyone about. Ask God to help you be humbly open, discerning, and compassionate. Ask God to help your child feel trust to open up with you honestly.

Date Questions

Offense Check: Is there anything in your heart that I do, have done, or have not done in the past that irritated, belittled, hurt, shamed, angered, or let you down that might hinder you from trusting me and opening up on our date today?

1. What is one of the most exciting or fun things you did in the last few months?

2. What has been one of the saddest things that has happened to you?

3. Has anyone ever offended you in a way that you got really mad or wanted to fight back?

4. Do you remember a time when one of us parents hurt your feelings that we never apologized for?

5. Loving correction does not need to be recanted here unless unnecessary hurt or shame has pierced a tender heart to discouragement or anger.

6. Has anyone ever jokingly verbalized something hurtful or made fun of you in a way that made you feel uncomfortable? Are there any ways you notice that still affect you?

7. What situations do you catch yourself trying to avoid?

8. Do you feel that God made you smart, wise, and skilled?

9. Do you like the way God made your gender, body, and personality?

10. Do you ever feel like you are not appreciated or welcomed by someone?

11. What are five adjectives that you would use to describe you?

🍦 What's a fun or sweet memory you have of Thanksgiving or Christmas?

🍦 If you could plan our next family vacation, what would be some of the places we'd go and things we'd do?

🍦 If you could add an appliance and piece of furniture to your room what would they be?

Closing Question

Do you have any questions you'd like to ask me?

Breaking Off the Lie in Prayer

Parent: Dear Lord, We bring to you the thing that happened to (child's name) _______________ during _______________. You saw how that made (child's name) _______________ feel very _______________.

   Child: Lord, I want to forgive (offenders) _______________ for making me feel so _______________. Show me Jesus, where you were and how I should think about what happened. Help me to receive your truth that I am (truth) _______________ instead of the lie that I am (negative emotion) _______________. Please heal the hurt and replace it with your strong love. In Jesus's powerful Name, Amen.

Date 7:
Preferred Learning Environment

4 Learning Styles: Visual, Auditory, Reflective and Kinesthetic to choose from.

See date question #9 to prepare items for a fun application.

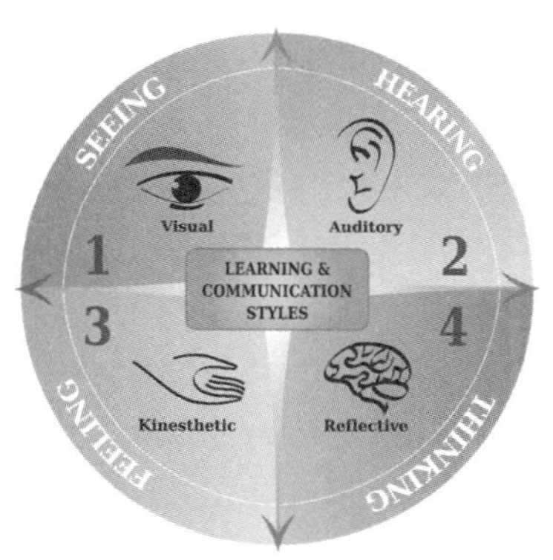

Our Story

I stood inspired to tears, sensing God calling me. The woman showing me the hand-sketched portraits on the wall had no idea why I was quiet and watery eyed. A desire to homeschool was being impressed on me as I witnessed parents quality relationships with their children. Now I felt it solidify as I stood looking over the heirloom orchard in this mother's quaint upstairs homeschooling sanctuary. Here, she and her children used their hands to create Egyptian pyramids and a mini Indian village as they learned history and science from a biblical worldview. The possibilities grabbed my interest.

In that one day, I was both impressed and humbled. The lovely older daughters served us all a nutritious lunch, which included broccomole, while their parents sat and invested time into me and my husband. The humbling part came when my boys would not listen during their LEGO spat, and the experienced mother kindly told me that if we were to follow through with homeschooling, we would need to get the first-time obedience thing down pat. So I got a calling and a correction all in one. This started my desire to homeschool and began my study of my children's different makeup and skills and how to "train [them] up in the way [they] should go" (Prov. 22:6, KJV).

Our oldest son does best with integrated combinations of physical, social, and verbal to enjoy his learning. Today as a grown-up, he has applied himself to reading self-help books, even though I used to have to require him to read a chapter a day (until he discovered The Hardy Boys series). He has played on organized teams of baseball, football, basketball, volleyball, and casual golf, not to mention horseback riding and heading up an annual cattle round-up in Colorado. Currently he has been involved in sharing the Gospel in a variety of cultures of children and youth ministry through drama and music as well. He influences through sensitivity of others and investing in relationships wherever he is. If ever I think someone was under-appreciated for his loyalty and kind serving in our home, it was him. Today he is considered a High S personality in DISC.

Our third born, I soon discovered, is self-motivated and prefers to know ahead what exactly will be expected of him so he can start early, conquer, and then reward himself with whatever he would like to do that day He would prefer to work in solitary environments before the others were up and around to distract his concentration. With children like this, it is easy to under-reward them for their diligence and responsibility. Quiet, uninterrupted with clear instructions is how this type of child executes best. We concluded he preferred a solitary, visual, and logical learning environment. Today he would be considered an Enneagram 1 with a wing of 2 and in DISC as a D I.

Our fourth born, who was the youngest for five years, was so determined to be independent, he refused my hand to cross the street at three years old. He excelled in every physical challenge, aiming to be as skilled as his older brothers. He seemed to be born with a natural vocabulary and knew how to spell English words without much studying or effort. I thank God that today he avoids competition and popular trends and enjoys paving different or difficult roads and studying prophecy. He is a self-taught musician, graphic artist, and recording studio engineer that teaches guitar and drum lessons to young children. This son very obviously enjoys solitary time and needs to be encouraged to join groups and open his heart in vulnerability. He loves to study and analyze without needing to share it with everyone.

Giving a child affirmation about who they are specifically, instead of comparing them to others, can bring our children to a rest from competition and needing others' affirmation. We lacked this at times. It is something that can be done by everyone in the child's life—mothers, babysitters, teachers, mentors, pastors—but somehow has the biggest impact coming from their own dad. Ask God to help you see this child's need and best atmosphere to prosper as you listen to their answers to these questions.

Schedule

Take time to look at your next month's schedule, discuss with your child the next possible date, and pencil it in the index calendar as well as your planner or phone calendar.

Date Questions

Offense Check: Is there anything in your heart that I do, have done, or have not done in the past that irritated, belittled, hurt, shamed, angered, or let you down that might hinder you from trusting me and opening up on our date today?

1. What is your favorite part of your day and why?

2. What frustrates you the most when you are trying to study?

3. How do you prefer to memorize something?

4. To learn more about a subject, would you rather read about it, have someone explain it, watch a video about it, or go and see it for real?

5. What distracts you most when you are trying to concentrate?

6. What helps you remember what you learned? Seeing and feeling something, writing about it, or talking about it with someone else?

7. Would you rather have your school desk in a room by yourself, in a classroom full of students, out on a deck, by a stereo in the living room, or in a quiet room with just your teacher?

🍦 Would you rather swim with dolphins or read a book about sharks?

8. Would you rather be in a chess tournament, spelling bee, trivia game, cooking and tasting party, historical field trip, bird watching field trip, science or space museum, participate in an Olympic challenge, or run in a local race?

9. For a fun extra activity, put an eye cover on them and have them use all the other senses but sight to guess the food and other various indoor and outdoor textured items you bring to them to smell, feel, taste, and listen to such as a watch or flies or bees in a jar.

10. If you listen to a teaching session, sermon, or podcast, what activity do you prefer to help you remember what you heard? Being at a place to see physically what they are illustrating, taking notes, drawing pictures, graphs, keeping data charts, discussing it with someone, typing quotes and notes on your phone or tablet, having visuals from the speaker, or picturing in your mind what they are saying with your own imagination?

 What are a few of your favorite wardrobe pieces?

Closing Question:

Do you have any questions you'd like to ask me?

Spoken Blessing

Lord, I pray for (child's name) _______________ when (he or she) is in school, Sunday school, and other learning opportunities with teachers and coaches such as (child's music or sports extracurricular classes) _______________________ that (he or she) can concentrate on learning the way you specifically have created (him or her) and not compare (himself or herself) with others as you equip (child's name) _______________ for who you have called (him or her) to be in this life. Give (him or her) grace to walk in humility instead of pride and faith instead of fear, worshiping you for how and in what pace you designed (him or her) to learn and develop for (his or her) calling in life. In Jesus's powerful Name, Amen.

What Might Be Their Life Message?

Our Story

Our nine-month-old daughter was just opening her eyes and taking in the odd scene of three ethnicities of hair-netted nurses adoring her bobbing blond spirals as they talked to the father holding her. The toddler pushed to sit up, taking in the strange fluorescent lighting of the Charlotte Hospital Pediatric Anesthesia Room. She relaxed upon discovering that her mother was right there, and when she received her routine morning cheek caresses from her ten-year-old sister whom she had shared a room with from birth.

We had decided to go through with our fifth child having cranial surgery to diffuse an area in her skull that had grown together prematurely before birth, causing a narrow, misshapen skull as it grew. The big sister had earnestly prayed for a sister for ten years before she was born, and she is still a great woman of faith in believing and seeking the Father with valuable petitions.

My journal reminded me how troubled she was by the thought of her baby sister having surgery in Charlotte while she played at a friend's house. She petitioned us tearfully that she should at least be there in the waiting room. Because of how she diligently cared for her and even had the baby's crib in her room, it seemed right to have her travel with us for the surgery.

Hard things that don't seem ideal such as tight spaces to raise a family, health difficulties, birth order, and relational sibling difficulties are a few of the things God gently uses to shape our children and our lives and develop characteristics such as empathy, humility, patience, understanding, willingness to serve, and bonding experiences for both us and our children.

With this same open, vulnerable heart, the older sister still relates to people loyally and personally today. Because they needed to share a room, as the years passed, the two sisters journaled at night, memorized Proverbs 31, went through the book *Lies Women Believe,* and discussed their struggles and highlights of their days even though there were nine years between them. They roomed and shared life together for sixteen years, and because of the nine-year gap between them, I feel like the big sister discipled her little sister about as much as we did.

I observed that this big sister's greatest strength in school was creative writing, even though she had some dyslexic symptoms when it came to spelling. We tried to encourage her in the strength and get a special program to help with spelling weakness. She was able to deal with the hurdle and publish her first book on father-daughter relationships before she got married. Her experience in mentoring her little shadow sister prepared her to walk through many open doors of opportunities in her twenties to influence and mentor other young girls in spite of having a more private personality

As a very young girl, I noticed she observed details of

what people wore and was very aware of clothes and hair that added some stress to our life. That attribute and trial also later turned into a positive as I watch her have opportunities to influence others through skin color analysis and teaching on beauty and modesty.

Another challenge during homeschooling was when we moved into a house that did not have a schoolroom and our students all sat at our dining room table and kitchen bar for their textbook work. For this oldest daughter, if there was any bread dough proofing or meal prep being done, she could hardly stay in her books when the hands-on food prep looked so much more appealing. This school year's trial also brought forth good fruit as I watched her food ministry as a teenager begin as she hosted celebrations as well as having weekly worship and sharing nights for single girls in our home. Have fun dreaming what the little things your children are attempting now may turn into for others someday!

Personal Reflections

Date Questions

Offense Check: Is there anything in your heart that I do, have done, or have not done in the past that irritated, belittled, hurt, shamed, angered, or let you down that might hinder you from trusting me and opening up on our date today?

 Who is your favorite aunt or uncle and why?

1. Would you rather help and encourage young children, poor people, unbelievers, inmates, abused children, orphans, elderly people, or sick people?

2. What other type of ministry would you enjoy being in?

 What is the nicest thing anyone ever said to you?

3. If someone gave you $10,000 to help people in need, what would you do with it?

4. Would you rather speak, sing, give presents, help, or pray with hurting people?

5. What burdens you most in this world?

6. Would you rather teach a class, serve refreshments, surprise someone with a gift, speak encouraging words in a card, offer a back rub, or organize a small group to meet weekly?

7. If you were to visit a sick person in the hospital, how would you try to encourage them?

   - By offering advice on what to do to get better? (teacher)
   - By offering to take care of their pets or things at the house while they are gone? (server)

- By encouraging them that God is with them in this? (exhorter)
- By preparing a nice gift and card or money for them? (giving)
- By rubbing their stiff muscles? (physical or medical help)
- By listening to them as they share the story of their accident? (listening, reporting, creating awareness)

8. What do you usually see as more of a need in your church that is not happening enough?

If you could be in a movie you've watched, who would you be?

9. What is something you try to be intentional about doing for other people?

10. In what way do you hope to impact the world and hope to be remembered for?

Is there a person of the opposite gender that you think are good-looking, talented, and would enjoy hanging out with?

Closing Question

Do you have any questions you'd like to ask me?

Child's Closing Prayer

Lord, you know the burden I have about __________ and the desire to help fill this need for someone to _______. If this is from You, God, and You want me to be a part of the solution in some way, someday, I trust you to prepare my heart for this and open the doors and provide the resources for me to accomplish bringing help and solution to this type of problem.

Parent's Prayer

Father God, you have made (child's name) ____________ and allowed things in (his or her) life that have formed the burden for _______________. I trust you to perfect the message and solution for this problem in my child and to open opportunities someday for (him or her) to accomplish and bring forth the message and resources needed to help this problem. We give to you the vision for _______________ and trust you with (his or her) future.

Schedule

Take time to look at your next month's schedule, discuss with your child the next possible date, and pencil it in the index calendar as well as your planner or phone calendar.

Responses to Remember

ORSE SHOW DAY

Date 9:

The Facts of Life

Our Story

During one of our ministry tours crossing the border into Canada, we planned to take a day and show the children Niagara Falls. My husband was aware our water tank was running low on the way north in our motor home. In this specific Swinger model motor home, the water pump could be shut off by the kitchen sink to keep it from continually running on a dry tank.

Unbeknown to us parents, one of our little travelers had tried to wash their hands in the tiny bathroom when no water came out and didn't think twice about leaving the faucet turned open. Meanwhile, Father and driver faithfully found a place to fill up our fresh-water tank en route. We arrived and parked at the Skyline Tower to give our children the experience of eating lunch in the huge rotating cylindrical restaurant at the top, which offers the full scope of the falls plummeting down either side of the bordering countries.

Right before we all exited the motor home for the exciting homeschool field trip, one of us turned the water pump back on to use the kitchen sink before we left. After riding the yellow buglike-looking elevator up to the top floor of the tower, we rationed two tourist-priced meals between the six of us. After taking in the awe of the height of our view above God's powerful water source of the northeast, we descended back to the parking level on the same yellow elevator.

What we found inside the motor home upon our return made us glad we were not omnipotent or we would have never enjoyed the time in the tower together. As we were oohing and awing at the great falls outside, there was a continual mini waterfalls running inside our very own motor home. Our full tank of fresh water flowed from the open bathroom faucet into the teeny sink, which over-flowed nicely into the nearby wastebasket, and then cas-caded out into the surrounding carpeted rooms until the tank was dry! We cried, laughed, and then sloshed into drying it all up the best we could to move on and hope to fill up that tank of water once again.

What Can I Do?

It was during an ordinary day of travel in that same Swing-er motor home, with our three elementary children and a toddler, where I had the opportunity to redeem an awk-ward moment into a beautiful teaching one.

I remember our first grader excitedly bringing a tampon she had discovered in a vanity cupboard up front asking loudly in front of the family, "Mom, what is this?" I looked at what she held, quickly put on a poker face that said "just boring normal stuff," and said, "Come and I will explain." I escorted her to the back room of the motor home. This was my first course in explaining to her more of a woman's reproductive ability and terminology. It was a perfect op-portunity to give her some knowledge without including the male's part of it yet, until she was ready for the next level.

I took the same approach several months later with all our school students. That opportunity was brought on once again as most teaching moments are: unplanned and inconvenient. Deuteronomy 6:7 says, "And thou shalt teach them diligently unto thy children, and shalt talk of them when thou sittest in thine house and when thou walkest by the way, and when thou liest down, and when thou risest up" (KJV). When we as parents stay in the mentality that our main role is to train, teach, and prepare them for independent living, then we will not look at these incidents as interruptions but opportunities for exactly why we stay or work at home and try to be with our children as much as possible.

I had been short of gracious and sweet in my responses to my children in my stressful circumstances that morning before school even started. I apologized to all of them for the way I had spoken to them, which seemed too obviously a monthly recurrence to me. I told them this is not an excuse for me to not be kind and loving, but I want to explain why it is more difficult for me to have this victory at certain times than others.

I explained to my children that I have a uterus where I carried them all in while they were being formed for nine months. I continued by saying that when that uterus does not get a new baby inside after the last one was born, that God empties the soft blood lining to put in fresh every month to prepare for the next baby, and when that process is going on, my body has to work harder and put out certain hormones and energy to accomplish this, and it affects my abilities to feel as well and be strong in other ways because of it. I gave them the terms, monthly or menstrual period, in case they ever hear of it, so they would not be ignorant but have a reverent, healthy view that God created a woman's cycle.

Following this conversation, I could honestly ask them to pray for me when I knew I was struggling mentally because of it, and they would be careful to be more cooperative and merciful to me. Wasn't that sweet of them? All I needed to say was, it is one of those days that my body is working hard and I am feeling a little sick, and they would do all they could to help and comfort me as they got older. To some of you, this may seem inappropriate since it had been such a hushed and secret subject in our parents' and grandparents' days. I respond with these questions: was it helpful to you as a child to not hear these things talked about from your parents? How could this information have helped you in your curiosity in when and how you did learn these things?

Before the Date

I encourage you to watch for teachable moments like those mentioned in the previous illustrations that seem perfectly natural. Your children need to hear these things from the best source: you.

Between six and ten years old, your child needs to have a safe place to go with all the new information and questions they have about how a baby is conceived, their own human anatomy, and what to expect when it will start changing. When these details are talked about freely as a good thing that God ordained, you open a door to your child learning about their bodies in a pure, positive manner.

Remember that a part of being a safe person is that you take care of any sin or shame that would keep you from openly talking about these private subjects without any guilt of your own diminishing your transparency with your child.

You may also want to take a moment to pencil in the blanks or on the side how you want to fill in the blanks on the prayer of blessing for this child personally before you go on the date.

Personal Reflections

Date Questions

Offense Check: Is there anything in your heart that I do, have done, or have not done in the past that irritated, belittled, hurt, shamed, angered, or let you down that might hinder you from trusting me and opening up on our date today?

🍦 Did you know what name we would have called you if you would have been the opposite gender?

1. Do you know which house we lived in when your mom was pregnant with you? *Tell them any positive details you remember that you as parents thought, discussed, hoped, and experienced during their pregnancy and birth.*

🍦 Have you ever watched a mother or animal in a live birth or on a video? Did you have any questions about the process?

🍦 Do you know how many months it takes for a baby to be fully grown and formed well enough in the womb to be born into the world and breathe on their own?

2. Have you heard or read any of these words and wondered what the definition is? Rectum, wet dream, bladder, urethra, vagina, scrotum, penis, masturbation, anus, semen, testicles, ovaries, orgasm, colostrum, seed, period, menstrual. *These and more are professionally explained on our website by Dr. Nic if you care to scan the QR code below.*

3. Have you or any one of your acquaintances ever crossed the line of what is respectful of each other's private body parts or acted in an inappropriate way? Can we make it right by apologizing or discussing it with them and/or their parents?

4. What message would you say a girl is giving when she indiscreetly shows a lot of her shape and skin in public? How is this subject affecting you currently?

🍦 What is a place you would love to win a free ticket to?

5. Since Jesus paid a high price with His blood to buy you from the kingdom of darkness and death, would you consider dedicating your body to Him and ask Him to protect and glorify His name through your giftings and skills?

6. What kind of books have you read parts of or the whole thing that include boy/girl relationships, dating, or romance? Was it portrayed in a healthy way, a sensual way, in an unrealistic or fictional manner? How did it leave you feeling?

7. Has anyone ever showed you, or have you ever found, accidentally or intentionally, pictures of unclothed people, indecent videos, or pornography?

🍦 If we would do a family TV dinner night, what movie and meal would you choose?

8. God made humans male and female with a beautiful purpose in mind and wants you to worship and glorify him with the body He gave you. Your body (or shell of your soul and spirit) will be maturing into a (young man or lady) in the upcoming years. What would you consider to be some pros and cons about your gender?

    Parent: if you dedicated this child as a baby to God, take this time to tell them about it.

9. God is very good at protecting His own things. Would you consider personally dedicating your body to Him as well?

🍦 What is a favorite memory you have of having a blast with friends?

10. Would you want to scan the QR code and hear more about this subject of your changing body and how a baby forms in the womb or ask me any questions about the facts of life or my own life when I was your age?

🍦 What is one of the most fun memories you have from the last few years?

Closing Question

Do you have any questions you'd like to ask me?

Spoken Blessing

Lord, thank you that (name of child) _____________ was born a (boy or girl) and how _______ and ______ (he or she) is. I like how (he or she) resembles _______ and acts a lot like _____ of (her or his) relations.

Lord please help (child's name) ________ to continue to build healthy relationships and discern what are appropriate relationship boundaries—intellectually, emotionally, and physically—in order to honor others as well as (his or herself) as the Temple of Your Holy Spirit. Help myself and (him or her) to have victory in our thought life to keep it pure before you. Help us to flee temptation and only view, listen to, and think upon "whatever things are true, whatever things are noble, whatever things are just, whatever things are pure, whatever things are lovely, whatever things are of good report, if there is any virtue and if there is anything praiseworthy" (Phil. 4:8, NKJV). We want to meditate on these types of things.

Responses to Remember

MIDDLE SCHOOL

AGES 11–14

POSITION OF ADULT ROLE:

It is expedient to relate to your child in a mature, respectful way whether they earn it or not. The goal is to build trust, friendship, and their self-confidence. During this stage of tweens, it is especially important for parenting not to feel demeaning. Remember how you felt at this age and recognize that they are transitioning from the innocence of childhood into the responsibility of adulthood. This process takes time, and many things are changing, including their bodies. Your role is to be a steadfast, secure person to walk with them. Stay in close communication as they face many new questions about who they are, what they believe, and whether or not they are enough. "Am I accepted by my peers?" is usually the biggest mind battle in this stage, and feelings of insecurity and discouragement are common as their hormones fluctuate in the growth spurt. Spend more time one-on-one with them to keep up with their daily battles.

Date 1:

Creating a Safe Place

When my friend was young, a much older, divorced guy sent her a private letter asking for a relationship. My friend's red flags all went off. This man knew her entire family, but she perceived that he was not a God-fearing man. She grew up in a God-professing home, church, and school and had goals to live purely and have a Godly husband and family.

The weight of this private conversation bore down on her conscience. Knowing he contacted her personally without consulting her parents, my friend summoned up the courage to go and tell her father. Although she worked with her dad every day, he was not in tune with what was going on in her life, nor currently protecting and caring for her heart. She felt very vulnerable before her father, telling him what this family friend was doing behind his back.

Days later, as she was wrestling and processing this

alone, she happened to overhear her father mentioning this man's attempts to his employees. The men responded with laughter and joking. At that moment, something tragic happened in my friend's heart. She felt so betrayed and uncared for by her own father that she asked herself a question she had never asked before. *Why am I saying no when no one cares if I give myself away? It's a joke to my father.*

When the heart hurts, we humans seem to have two choices:

1. To face the reality of how wounded and misunderstood we felt by someone we thought loved us and take our grief to God for help.

OR

2. To harden our hearts and stuff the reality of pain away. We might "toughen up" or turn to a new way to cope and overcome the negative emotions with a positive emotion, seeking pleasure, approval, accomplishments, or thrills of any kind.

Sadly, that was the last time this daughter would confide in her father about personal struggles or the boy subject. As people with feelings, we don't usually keep subjecting ourselves to someone who has paraded our personal battles as a joke to others. The father had no idea that his daughter overheard or that it broke her heart and trust. But our Heavenly Father sees all this, and for this we are grateful. He knows. He doesn't forget. He cares about the parent and the child.

When I think of the words of Jesus, I am greatly comforted for the world's neglected and abused children, but tremble for the adults through whom the offenses come. Matthew 18:6–7 says, "But whoso shall offend one of these little ones which believe in me, it were better for him that a millstone were hanged about his neck, and that he were drowned in the depth of the sea. Woe unto the world because of offenses! for it must needs be that offenses come; but woe to that man by whom the offense cometh!" (KJV), and again in verse 10, "Take heed that ye despise not one of these little ones; for I say unto you, that in heaven their angels do always behold the face of my Father which is in heaven."

I thank God for Jesus's accomplishments that can cover and mend the family issues and heart pain as old as Eden. In verse 11, Jesus followed the serious warning with "for the Son of Man has come to save that which is lost!" Hallelujah! That includes us parents who offend those we love, sometimes unaware of what we are doing. We can tap into Him for both our own parent wounds and for grace to empower our current parenting methods and their quality.

It breaks my heart to relate that my friend experienced feeling unknown, uncared for, and judged. After her heart questioned why she would say no when no one cared, she did not experience loving, positive answers. She did choose to give herself away, and her future would include losses of morals and trust. She felt taken advantage of, uncared for, unprotected, and alone.

We are aware that this young lady could have been spared from many of these hurdles if someone had taken time to know her, show her the worth God places on her, and care for her heart and well-being. We are not casting stones. Her parents probably had never experienced that kind of care from their own parents either. There is grace and mercy for everyone.

Each of us parents have our own cultural lies and wounds from the past that require much divine help! We each choose whether we stay soft and vulnerable or harden ourselves to compromise. Jesus offers help and healing for every individual.

What Can I Do?

As a parent or mentor, have there been any areas where our joking or responses to younger people's acknowledgment of life circumstances has not felt safe? Have we prompted them to close off from us in the future?

I am happy to say that my friend in the earlier story is seeking God's face and has found revolutionary healing and grace for the past experiences. This friend, myself, and so many others I know were able to find healing by applying the concepts Jesus taught and making it practical.

Your Own Heart Care

It can be helpful to process and use tools similar to a few in the index of this book, such as asking, "Why am I triggered?" and providing heart care to our soul wounds. Our children can experience a very different childhood than we did. Instead of continuing the vicious cycle of hurt people hurting people, healed parents can give what they did not receive as children to their own children. This begins when we embrace and receive those things, by faith, from our Heavenly Father first.

I love the opportunity of improving in depth, quality, and genuine love as we become more whole parents. We are a generation without excuse because of having ample access to so much learning and proven methods taught in all forms at our fingertips!

Ask yourself: did I feel safe and cared for growing up? If not, why not? Take time to reflect on your own. You can then determine action steps to become a safe place for the next generation. You are influencing that generation for good or bad, depending on your involvement or lack of it. Absence is a way to not love our children on purpose. Be encouraged that you can totally change the culture of your home by being intentional. Desiring to learn brings life-giving, transformational change.

Personal Reflections

Date Questions

 What is your favorite drink at a coffee shop?

1. What was one of your biggest disappointments lately?

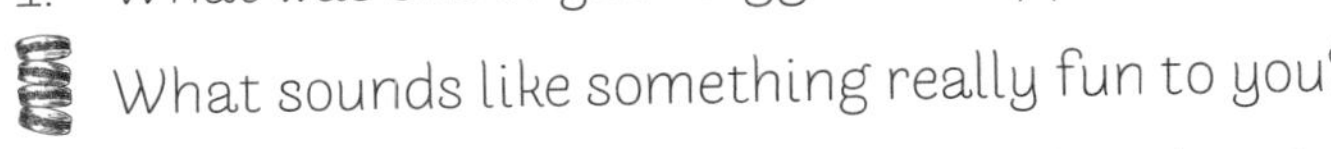 What sounds like something really fun to you?

2. Is there a time of the day that you dread and why?

3. Is one day of the week better or worse than others to you?

4. Do you ever battle loneliness?

5. Is there something you remember that we as parents have promised or mentioned that we haven't done yet?

6. Who do you trust the most with things in your heart, and what is it about them that makes you feel safe?

7. Was there a time you felt misunderstood by me?

8. Is there an instance in your mind where I hurt your feelings and didn't apologize?

9. Have you ever felt unprotected by us as parents?

10. Is there something you enjoy that you wish we as parents would take more interest in?

Would you enjoy meeting on another date, and if so, where would you want to go?

What is one of your favorite memories of the last year, and why did it stand out to you?

Testimony Video

Closing Question

Now, it's your turn if you want to ask me any questions.

Spoken Blessing

After hearing you say how you felt ______________ when
I ________________, I want to ask if you can find it in your
heart to forgive me. I hadn't realized
how it caused you to feel and never
meant to ____________ you. Thank
you for your honesty.

*Take time to look at them while you
tell them something you have noticed
that they did a good job at or were
faithful in carrying out and that you
enjoyed this time with them alone.*

Schedule

Take time to look
at your next month's
schedule, discuss with
your child the next
possible date, and pencil
it in the index calendar
as well as your planner
or phone calendar.

Responses to Remember

Routines and Relationships

Parent Tip

When my oldest two children entered double-digit ages, their relationship began to show signs of strain. The brother felt too old to play pretend games anymore. They both became more aware of the opposite gender and what their peers considered cool. When they wanted to relate, but the conversations felt awkward and sparse, they would often turn to teasing or challenging each other verbally.

One day I asked them both to have a seat beside me on the couch. I explained that I am glad they both have friends their age and that it is important. Even so, the only relationships that will for sure last and be there ten, twenty, and thirty years from now are family ones. I explained that they are both maturing and their interests are changing. The things they do and discuss together will change with seasons, but staying connected through the process is worthwhile and very important. I pointed out how they have turned into a little young man and woman and should treat each other with that kind of respect.

I tried to encourage my son that it's an advantage to have a sister close to his age. He can practice how to best relate to girls, take time to ask his sister questions, and listen to her opinions and thoughts. He can ask her what she thinks about his hair, clothes, and shoes and vice versa.

I told his sister that she can have a head start in knowing how boys think by asking her brother questions and learning to respect and understand him. I encouraged them to find new activities to do together such as table games, outdoor sports, or going to the park and sharing good talks, walks, or bike rides together. I told them they have always been close, and I look forward to teaching them both to drive and releasing them to more independent adventures and experiences in life together. To cherish their relationships and protect it above their outside relationships, having each other's backs instead of tearing each other down.

Later on, we established a family rule that if someone speaks negatively to or about someone in the family, they need to speak three positive attributes about them. Those two oldest went on to draw closer as they went from teens to twenties and took in weeks of training for children's ministry and school of music together as well as traveling to India, Africa, and Asia where they ministered and taught at a refugee camp together.

All relationships affect our future thinking. On this date, listen to see which relationships are strained and see if you can exhort your child in any helpful way to mend or enhance those relationships.

Quote: "Could it be that one of the reasons that our nation is under curse is because of Malachi 4:6? 'He will turn the hearts of the parents to the children, and the hearts of the children to the parents, or else I will come and strike the land with destruction'" (NIV). - Dave

Date Questions

Offense Check: Is there anything in your heart that I do, have done, or have not done in the past that irritated, belittled, hurt, shamed, angered, or let you down that might hinder you from trusting me and opening up on our date today?

What would be your favorite ride, show, and food at a fair or carnival?

1. Do you feel judged wrongly or misunderstood in our family?

2. Who do you feel most comfortable to hang out with in our family?

3. What tends to irritate or discourage you at home?

What pet would you enjoy having if money and space were not a problem?

4. What would help you enjoy being home more?

5. What is something we could do more often as a family that would help bring us closer?

6. Have you ever felt like we as parents are showing any favoritism?

7. What would you consider one of the coolest things we have done to make good memories as a family?

8. What are one or two standards we could establish in our home that would be helpful and prevent problems between us?

What is the latest book or article you read or podcast you listened to?

9. Do you have any suggestions or changes that we could make for getting everyone involved in home upkeep and daily jobs?

10. As a teenager, you have a lot of influence. Would you be willing to write out a blessing note of encouragement to give to several or one of your siblings this next week?

Closing Question

Now it's your turn if you want to ask me any questions.

Spoken Blessing

Using any personal pet name you call them, encourage your child what an important individual they are in the makeup of your family. Share some things you notice about them that are an asset to the home.

Prayer over the child: Thank you, Lord, for bringing (child's name) _____________ into our family. Thank you for how (he or she) relates well with _________________ when _______________ and contributes to our family relationships with (his or her) (specific character trait, virtue or personality trait) ________________________________.
I bless (him or her) with grace and patience to respond to _______________, which is hard at times and thank you for this special time we have had together.

Schedule

Take time to look at your next month's schedule, discuss with your child the next possible date, and pencil it in the index calendar as well as your planner or phone calendar.

Responses to Remember

Maintaining a
Clear Conscience

Parent Tip

At this stage, your child may start comparing what they were taught and saw modeled in their family to the ways people around them live out their faith. This is a natural, healthy, and necessary process in order for your child to form their own belief system. You want your child to have reason to follow convictions and applications of principles for the sake of their relationship with God, not just for their parents' sake.

As they near puberty, you may also be dismayed by your child doing something you associate with an immoral lifestyle. Take time to inquire of their knowledge of the harm or evil association, and then explain the intent or origin to them. This can be done without making them feel blamed or ashamed. Even tweens are innocent until they have been educated on why something is unacceptable. They need your guidance.

When one of our daughters was a preteen, I was surprised to see the poses she and her friends were striking for photos, forming puckered "kissy lips" and placing hands on angled hips. I explained the message that could portray to the opposite gender and why ladies might pose that way with an agenda. She was shocked at the thought of communicating anything suggestive or immoral. Like most girls, she acknowledged they just wanted to be beautiful. I was surprised by her reception, innocence, and intentionality to avoid any questionable poses in the future.

These moments are opportunities for you to kindly activate your child's conscience for a lifetime. You can explain what is respectful and what is not without making them feel guilty. If you can do this as a safe, bonding experience, it will open the door for them to feel welcome and want to come to you with bigger, more detrimental things going on in their life.

By walking with your children through their relationship struggles in a healthy, biblical manner, you are preparing and teaching the next generation of Christians to walk in honor with all people so that the world may see who Christ is.

Guilt on your child's conscience is a kind reminder to come before God for forgiveness and cleansing. You can help them see this by offering an open door to communicate troubling memories. The second step is from Matthew 18, relating to any other people involved. Help your child discern whether they should go to anyone else that was involved in the confessed incident or offense to make things right. This shows them the importance of restitution between people as well as with God. If you deem it necessary, you can offer to go with your child to ask for forgiveness of the other child, without any accusation (with that child's parental agreement and presence).

If the child confesses something shameful that bothers their conscience, no matter how minuscule or big, remember to smile kindly and take time to lead them in prayer of confession. Name the sin to God out loud and ask God to please forgive them in order to clear their conscience of the offense.

Discipline and loving consequences should be only for direct disobedience to a clear instruction, never for innocent curiosity or failure to perform well.

If punishment is a result of honest confessions, you are communicating that it is better for future failures and sins to be kept secret from you. Remember how your Heavenly Father responds to your confession of sins. Natural consequences of sowing and reaping may be, and often are, a result of sinful actions, but mercy flows from God to us during them.

Remember to take care of anything on your mind first that would hinder you from freely focusing on your child. Then prepare to listen kindly and earnestly to what they are trying to communicate from their heart without interrupting. Have fun and relish your time together!

Personal Reflections

Date Questions

Offense Check: Is there anything in your heart that I do, have done, or have not done in the past that irritated, belittled, hurt, shamed, angered, or let you down that might hinder you from trusting me and opening up on our date today?

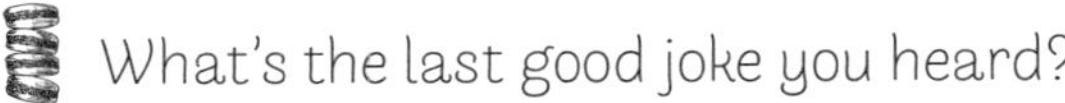 What's the last good joke you heard?

1. Are there any specific stresses or fears in your life right now?

2. Do you frequently feel lonely, angry, discouraged, afraid, or sad inside? If so, do you know what circumstances tend to bring these feelings?

3. What type of knowledge or perspectives do your friend groups have about the subjects of smoking, drinking, and drugs? Have you been offered or tried any form of them?

4. Have you been tempted to join in or do something else that you don't really want to do?

   If someone said they would buy you a truck for their tax write-off, what brand and model would you choose?

5. Has anyone done anything embarrassing or shameful to you that made you feel disrespected?

6. Have you done something to someone else that wasn't respectful or appropriate?

   What's a favorite meal of yours?

7. Do you know what masturbation means? Has anyone talked to you about it?

What is one music artist or group you would enjoy seeing live?

8. Has anyone told you facts or something that happened that you are not supposed to tell anyone but you wish you could erase?

9. Did you know that the knowledge of others' secret sins can keep you from feeling free and at peace? (Leviticus 16:8–10 in the Old Testament says carrying their sins makes you a scapegoat.)

What are some of your favorite activities outdoors?

10. Are there any toxic memories or dreams coming to your mind that you want to forget and be rid of?

If you've been to an amusement park, what was the best and worst ride you went on?

What is the most delicious donut you've sunk your teeth into?

Closing Question

Now it's your turn if you want to ask me any questions.

Spoken Blessing

Take time to face your child and make eye contact. Speak encouragement and affirmation into them with kindness.

I have seen you maturing more into a grown-up and appreciate you trusting me with your stresses, secrets, and the hard things in your life. I want to be there for you, sharing life's disappointments as well as the highlights!

I would love to help further free you from some of these thoughts by helping you verbally give them to God so you are no longer carrying them as a hindrance to your freedom of mind.

Child's Prayer of Release: Father, I give to you the knowledge of (something bothering their conscience) _________________ that I still have in my head as well as the visuals of (pictures still in the mind) _________ and memory of (bothering thoughts of the scenario) __________. I give these memories to you and ask you to cleanse my mind by the blood of Jesus and say to Satan, I renounce any involvement in this and want no part of this or anything linked to it in my life. I pray in the name of Jesus Christ our Lord.

Parents' Closing Scripture Prayer: Lord, as you prayed in John 17:11 for your disciples, I pray for this young one. "For those of us who are in the world, still: Keep through your name, those whom you have given me that they may be one, as we are one. I do not pray that you should take them out of the world, but you should keep them from the evil one" (John 17:15, NKJV).

Schedule

Take time to look at your next month's schedule, discuss with your child the next possible date, and pencil it in the index calencar as well as your planner or phone calendar

Responses to Remember

Skills to Steward

I add the creamy whipped topping and dust red sprinkles over six mugs on the serving tray, steaming with the frothed Trim Healthy Mama dandy blend to delight my family having a cyber party downstairs. Upon returning, the seventh will be placed by the couch corner where I will have some me-time with my feet up, going through Pinterest, snail-mail catalogs and coupons, or waiting emails and messages. I voluntarily make and carry these drinks to my family, even while feeling frustrated that I have been working ever since the supper dishes.

Do any parents relate? My natural method of hinting for help can often feel like an unhappy mother's guilt trip to my family members. They feel like innocent victims of my sudden displeasure, while in my head I am the victim with the right motive and they are insensitive to my needs. My natural response as I pass through the room they are sitting in, picking up empty glasses and leftover snack remnants, was to share some things I still needed to do and maybe how tired or weary I was. To my husband, that sounded like ungratefulness and complaining and gave him no desire to offer to help me out. I have learned a better way, but it still doesn't come naturally or feel fair or fun.

Whether we like it or not, at times, waiting for commercial time or asking for them to excuse our interruption, standing waiting until they finish, or sending a message on their phone is a way to inject necessary communication or home maintenance delegation.

When I ask for specific help and clarify my needs, it keeps my family unified. On the other hand, passive-aggressive comments can leave them feeling accused. Having a family "To Do" list on the refrigerator for the week is another wise way for them to fit it in between their duties and social life. By having each one initial which one they are planning on doing or have done, you can also see who is carrying their fair share and who isn't.

Before the Date

Whether it's to earn a horse, an accessory, cell phone, kayak, or moped, this is a stage of life where many tweens want to work for money to accomplish goals they are dreaming about. No matter how you have allowances or side-job earnings set up, they can be learning and conquering many skills and chores around the house by now and should be an asset not a liability. A mother of twelve told me once that if I am worn-out tired, I am probably not delegating well. Ouch. That deflates the victim mentality and calls me to see how I can be a better CEO of our home by stewarding the work and assigning kind dividends of responsibility.

One thing we tried off and on was having each child responsible to keep their own room and one other room spotless all week long. You will need to address rules on accusation versus picking up kindly after each other. The inward smile evokes when suddenly they take on the battle with clutterers instead of you.

Do clutter, dirty fingerprinted doors, and overgrown landscaping stress you? Assign a drawer to the "organizer child" and a bucket of Murphy's suds to the "scrubber child" and pruning shears to "the artistic one" for a Martha Stewart Makeover.

Take this date time to listen to discern how you might make "work seem like an art" to this child or whether it's time they roll up their sleeves and do it whether it's their gig or not.

Personal Reflections

Date Questions

Offense Check: Is there anything in your heart that I do, have done, or have not done in the past that irritated, belittled, hurt, shamed, angered, or let you down that might hinder you from trusting me and opening up on our date today?

1. What are some things you dream of accomplishing?

2. What is a responsibility around the home that you think you could be trusted with currently?

3. What business sounds like an interesting place to work for you?

4. Are you more interested in learning more about music, sports, speaking, writing, nature, landscaping, painting, building, designing things, or something else not mentioned here?

5. Would you feel more accomplishment from making something yourself or saving up enough to buy it new?

6. Would you rather we take you to a concert, play, hiking, sports game, museum, bird watch, canoeing, art class, a new local library, or rodeo?

7. Do you prefer when our house is orderly and everyone is quietly doing their own thing or when we as a family are doing an activity together and the work is not all done?

8. Does it bother you more if someone doesn't get the details right in telling a story or when people forget to ask questions about others and just do most of the talking?

9. Would you rather take part in a science experiment, cooking class, music lesson, Christmas play, trip to a museum, aquarium, greenhouse, pottery class, or nature hike?

10. What is a position or job you would enjoy having at school or in church?

    Who is someone in history you admire?

Closing Question

Now it's your turn if you want to ask me any questions.

Spoken Blessing

Pray out loud with them about their future and ask God to open up neat opportunities for them to be fulfilled in using the gifts and skills they are acquiring in jobs and ministry.

Schedule

Take time to look at your next month's schedule, discuss with your child the next possible date, and pencil it in the index calendar as well as your planner or phone calendar.

Responses to Remember

Studying Their Personality

Parent Tip

What a morning. My heart is beating fast. My brother was out in the motor home putting on his tie when we were supposed to start our family drama called "Red Tie" for the church audience. Mother ran out, the audience was waiting in silence, Duane Mullet finally grabbed a few CD recordings and did some announcements. Tension. Not good at all. But we shall laugh later. In fact, I feel a smile bursting on my face as I think of it all. Ah well.

This is one excerpt from our daughter's writings over the years in the red bound journal she carried as a prop in the aforementioned *Red Tie Skit*. We performed this skit when our children were school-aged and our family shared in churches and prisons.

Picture the personalities you have in your family and the strengths and weaknesses of each one of those personalities as you read more of our own family dynamics and issues recorded from the sister's view.

Another page in this book reads:

This Red Tie book was purchased at Fred Meyer in Newport, Oregon. It shall contain all things random, since the only time it shall be written in is during the six minutes which I pretend to be recording important information for the resort. No bloopers have taken place thus far in the drama. We are at a Seventh Day Adventist Church with a sprinkling of Mennonites throughout.

I take the no bloopers back. A certain brother failed to open the door for "Bill Blotz" to enter through at the end thus I was taken off guard and lamely tried to say: "Your name's in the book now!" a bit late. This brother, known in the skit as "Delaw," and I had it out about it later. Usually he doesn't admit he's in the wrong but expected me to open the door instead and commented that I must have no reflexes. Eye roll. Oh brother.

During yet another performance of this skit, she penned:

Well now how great and wonderful a gift to be with these people here in Columbiana, Ohio. Thank you Jesus for this privilege. Thanks that people still laugh at the "Red Tie Joke Lines." Thanks that my brothers are so good at acting and studly. Help me honor them. Teach me to honor them. Help that oldest brother to stop laughing between his lines. That silly boy. The next brother may or may not be my favorite brother, however it is true that he is a stud. Please allow your kingdom work to be accomplished through us. May we be nothing so you can be all.

Another page, the little sister who could barely spell yet scribbled:

> I do not like these *tites* that I am wearing, they are itchy *to.*

The last quote recorded from big sister tells you how my husband always emphasized resolving any conflict or differences before we go in public and try to minister.

> It's a tremendous good accountability to have a service every night. One cannot keep secret sins or tension between each other or God, or we know our ministry would be put to naught. Sometimes that accountability is hard when you need time to process and deal with things but need to apologize quickly and go update, depending on Him.

As you prepare to hear from this specific personality in your home on this date, remember to watch for ways to see the good parts of it that benefit people around them. Lovingly advise them how to overcome the traits that tend to irritate others. Have fun and celebrate who God made them!

Personal Reflections

Date Questions

Offense Check: Is there anything in your heart that I do, have done, or have not done in the past that irritated, belittled, hurt, shamed, angered, or let you down that might hinder you from trusting me and opening up on our date today?

1. Do you consider yourself outgoing or reserved?

2. When you want to relax and enjoy yourself, do you prefer to be with people or alone?

3. Would you rather be in charge of a project and have others help you or have someone else be in charge and you assist them?

4. What frustrates you the most in a group project?

5. Do you consider yourself more of a dreamer, visionary, server, leader, manager, encourager, teacher, or someone who mercifully cares for others?

6. Do you tend to think more about the things happening right now or about what could happen in the weeks, months, and years ahead?

7. If you need to finish a project, do you get more accomplished all alone or with a partner, in a quiet space or with music on?

8. What is your idea of a fun night?

9. What are some ways being born the _____ (oldest, middle, youngest) child in our family affected you?

10. What do you see as advantages and disadvantages about being born where you were in our family?

 If you could fly anywhere for a week, where would you want to go?

Closing Question

Now it's your turn if you want to ask me any questions.

Spoken Blessing

I want to say that I like who God made you to be and don't want you to compare yourself to other personality types. I pray you can be celebrated and enjoy how God created and designed you to be unique. There is only one version of you. May God give you wisdom and compassion for the rest of the family as you accept your birth order and the important role you play in our family. You bring a healthy balance of viewpoints with your ability to___________ and at times ___________. We need that. We need you.

Schedule

Take time to look at your next month's schedule, discuss with your child the next possible date, and pencil it in the index calendar as well as your planner or phone calendar.

Responses to Remember

Date 6:
Love Language

Parent Tip

A church attender may have been a bit curious to watch the scene of our children during their father's sermon. From the pew behind us, they could have noticed one of the children giving a sibling a hand rub or back scratch. Two others may have been passing notes that created stifled giggles or rolling eyes.

Our children sit through more services in one month than many children do in a year. If we are having a week of revivals at one church, they may experience sitting through anywhere from eight to ten services in one week, hearing similar sermons and stories from their father month after month. When we have two weeks of community tent meetings, that number more than doubles. Realizing the commitment this requires, we as parents allow activities during these services that they would not participate in during our home Sunday morning services (and we do give them breaks to go out to our bus during a sermon and have a night or morning off). During these consecutive, long periods of sitting, I have watched my children begin to unconsciously meet each other in their Love Languages™ from *The 5 Love Languages: The Se-*

cret to Love that Lasts by Dr. Gary Chapman.

Some Love Languages™ showing up during these services are Physical Touch™ through the hand rubs and back or arm scratches, Words of Affirmation™ or Quality Time™ in the form of sarcasm, art, humor, or teasing via notes, as well as Giving Gifts™ through surprise art or origami paper creations made for someone.

Today all of us are adults, and we have come up with ways to bond and affirm each other as we travel from destination to destination. Often planting yourself on the carpet in front of a family member sitting on the couch for half an hour of travel can result in a stiff shoulder kink being worked loose. We can't hold adult children who've outgrown us in our laps anymore, but moments like this can meet the Love Language™ of Physical Touch™ .

Sometimes before arriving to conduct a service or concert somewhere, we meet for prayer up in the front of the bus to include the driver. During this intercession for the upcoming event, we often pray blessings on individual family members' parts in the upcoming service, which can be a form of Words of Affirmation™ in their gifting and contribution of their skills. After the services, it is not uncommon for us to take time to be together and discuss the audience, the feel of the event, and how God helped each one in the expected roles, which comes also as Quality Time™ and Words of Affirmation™.

As you can see, it is not difficult through a few family habits and established traditions to cover each child's needs or hit their Love Language™ whether you have studied them for each one yet or not. What are your family rituals and habits? Where can you make space for time together and create moments that might meet individual needs?

It is true that there are other factors that play into whether a person or child *feels* loved or not when someone attempts to show love even in your favorite ways, called your Love Language™.

You and Your Child's Heart Care

A few reasons why you, your spouse, or your child may not be able to feel loved in spite of receiving love in their personal Love Language™:

- They have formed a filter that keeps them from receiving love because of a lie in their past that felt true. It could be thoughts of feeling unworthy, unwanted, uninvited, dumb, unaccepted, unlike others, less than, etc. These kinds of thoughts can make us a bag of holes. People can pour love into us, even in our personal Love Language™, and it seems to drain directly out through the holes.
- The person had to put up guards around their heart to protect their feelings from being smashed and has not felt safe to put them down since.
- If their positive and negative emotions were not nurtured, cared for, or celebrated when they were young, they have never learned to let themselves be honest with what they feel. Instead, they are used to stuffing emotions as bad things and trying to keep them secret and under control.

The Five Love Languages™:
Physical Touch™, Quality Time™, Words of
Affirmation™, Giving Gifts™, Acts of Service™

Date Questions

Offense Check: Is there anything in your heart that I do, have done, or have not done in the past that irritated, belittled, hurt, shamed, angered, or let you down that might hinder you from trusting me and opening up on our date today?

1. If someone new moved in and would want to become friends with you, what would be the best way for them to do that?

2. If I wanted to show you how much I care about you, how can I best communicate that to you?

Who are some athletes you admire?

3. What are some ways you try to encourage or appreciate your current friends?

4. What are two Love Languages™ that your friend might have that you would have a harder time relating to as necessary and trying to show them love in that way?

What are your favorite two subjects in school and why?

5. Who are two people in your life that you feel the most love from and why?

6. If someone wants to give you a real meaningful gift, what type of gift would speak your language?

What would be your favorite ride, show, and food at a fair or carnival?

7. How do you tend to hear from God? Through Scripture verses, songs, pictures He gives you, nature, gifts, songs, protection, provision, stories, dreams, visions, analogies, or any other way? *This may be a hint of your child's Love Language™ as well.*

8. What are three things people do that make you feel disrespected or uncared for?

 If I would give you thirty dollars to pick up food for a road trip, what would you buy?

9. Would you rather I surprise you with a thoughtful, personal gift; a back, foot, or scalp rub; a note with encouragement of who you are; help you with a project you are doing; or have a fun time spent somewhere together?

10. What is something you have heard that a parent has done for their child that would sound exciting or very meaningful to you?

Who have been your favorite mentors, teachers, instructors, or coaches you've had so far?

Closing Question

Now it's your turn if you want to ask me any questions.

Do you desire to know more details about your family's Love Languages™? Take the test at https://5lovelanguages.com/ quizzes/love-language or see Gary Chapman's book, The 5 Love Languages of Teenagers.

Closing Conversation and Prayer Suggestion

If needed, ask your child to forgive you for not realizing what means the most to them when you are trying to love and care for them. Follow up by asking them to pray for you as parents to be able to understand them better and try to remember how to best care for them by loving them in their personal Love Language™.

Schedule

Take time to look at your next month's schedule, discuss with your child the next possible date, and pencil it in the index calendar as well as your planner or phone calendar.

Responses to Remember

Spiritual State of Being

Our Story

One morning I overheard my five-year-old daughter sharing the plan of salvation, with all the graveness of burdens for lost souls, to her four-year-old brother in the sandbox. We don't think she gained a convert that hour, but she certainly planted a seed. Somewhere in the next months or year, during one of his dad's Gospel sermons in a prison, that little brother asked me to kneel with him by our pew in the back during the altar call. He received Jesus's gift of salvation at a very young age.

My husband and I have been zealous and attempted to share the Gospel and Jesus's love wherever we go as we feel led. However, since we were saved at nineteen and twenty-one years old, we cannot relate to evangelizing as young as our children have. They challenge us with their sweet burden for the lost and their kind and giving hearts toward those less fortunate as we travel. It is good and refreshing, while simultaneously challenging, when the knowledge of Heaven and Hell in eternity dawns on our children (or anew on an adult) and they live in a radically different way because of it. That is the Gospel.

Your Story

What was your spiritual knowledge, experience, or temperature when you were a tween? Mine was very basic: I knew there was a God who created everything and that Jesus came to love and suffer. But I didn't know how it related to me personally. In the Parent Tips of the younger ages, I shared my exposure to Mailbox Club stories that shared how to get saved. However, because of what I heard in our church services, I assumed we did not believe that way, so I never applied it to my own life.

One way God changed some of my faulty theology was by speaking to me through a very dramatic, supernatural dream. As I became more aware of my own fleshly, sinful tendencies and carried personal guilt, I had a healthy fear of God but didn't know how to get rid of the guilt of my sin. I used to think that if I were to be dying, I would quickly ask Jesus to forgive me and all would be fine. In my dream, Jesus came back to earth, down through the clouds. In awe and reverence and fearful dread, I quickly tried to pray that He would forgive me—but it was too late, it didn't work!

I was terrified that night and for many days ahead, realizing I was wrong and yet had another chance. What puzzles me is why I didn't tell someone about my dream and ask them what I should or could do. Who would you have gone to spiritually when you were just about to become a teenager? I should have gone to my parents. I often wonder what they would have said or encouraged me to do if I had at that point. I went on living with that fear of His return into my unsaved teen years until someone explained what I could do to be saved at nineteen years old.

Personal Reflections

I hope on this date:

1. You will take time to personally share with your child your own spiritual journey and mention where you were personally with Jesus at their age.
2. Your child can feel cared for and not threatened by these questions concerning their faith or belief.
3. That your interest and discussion on spiritual matters in their life would encourage and help them to take the next big step of faith and grow to a deeper, more daily and rooted relationship with God because of your time and care.
4. If your child has not responded to Jesus's gift of salvation yet, this could be their time in a quiet, safe place with you.

Before the Date

Ask God to draw yourself and your child's heart to Himself and to give you discernment how to facilitate this date in accordance with the Holy Spirit's guidance.

Date Questions

Offense Check: Is there anything in your heart that I do, have done, or have not done in the past that irritated, belittled, hurt, shamed, angered, or let you down that might hinder you from trusting me and opening up on our date today?

- Would you rather drive an eighteen-wheeler, slingshot, sailboat, hang glider, or motorcycle?
- What's the funniest pickup line you remember?

1. How would you describe Jesus to someone who never heard of him?

2. I know it's hard for a human to picture God. From what you have heard and read and believe to be true about God, how would you describe Him to someone who trusts in idols or believes in many gods?

3. Is there a thing, activity, or person in your life that means so much to you that it or they could begin competing with your time and attention for God?

4. If you talk to God, when and where and what about do you pray?

5. When did you start believing enough to talk to Him about your personal things?

- Would you rather go skydiving, scuba diving, or bull riding?

6. When and where were you if you ever prayed the sinner's prayer of forgiveness and asked in faith for Jesus to save you?

7. If you did pray the sinner's prayer, how did you feel afterward? Did you experience or notice anything new or different in the following days that you can remember?

8. If you would pass away in your sleep tonight, do you know where your soul would go?

9. Do you want to rededicate your life to God for assurance that you are at peace with where you will spend eternity?

10. Would you be willing to dedicate your body to God for His glory and for Him to protect it and work through you for His Kingdom?

What country or culture would intrigue you to go visit?

If you could eat whatever you wanted for breakfast, lunch, and dinner for one day, what would those meals look like?

Closing Question

Now it's your turn if you want to ask me any questions.

If child has never prayed to receive Christ as Savior:

Dear God, thank you that you have watched over me all of my childhood up until now. I realize that I am a sinner in need of a Savior or I would deserve to be in Hell for eternity. I believe that you sent your son Jesus to die in my place so I can be saved from hell and be forgiven by His shed blood on the cross. Please forgive me for all my sins, cleanse me, and put your Holy Spirit within me. I repent from my own way and want to be born again and baptized into your Holy Kingdom. Please write my name in the Book of Life and fill me with Your Spirit and spiritual gifts. Thank you so much for choosing me to be adopted into your family!

Rededication for salvation prayer sample:

Dear God, You heard when I asked for your forgiveness earlier, but now I just want to come before you again to be sure my sins are under the blood. I believe your Word that says, "God sent His son into the World that the world through Him might be saved." I personally believe that Jesus was your son and born from a virgin to come and die for me so I can go to Heaven. Can you please forgive me for all my sins and in-iquities and cleanse me by Jesus's precious blood? I believe the verse that says, "And whoever's name was not found in the Book of Life was cast into the Lake of Fire" (Rev. 20:15, KJV).

Schedule

Take time to look at your next month's schedule, discuss with your child the next possible date, and pencil it in the index calendar as well as your planner or phone calendar.

Responses to Remember

Life Message

I looked at the Family Fun magazine article a little more closely as I punched a hole through the cardboard box. Eventually the black-construction-papered tire with its shiny foil rim was added onto the hand-painted sports car. For me as a stay-at-home, mostly domestics-focused, homeschool mom, planning themed or beautiful events at our home brought some fun into my repetitive labors. It was during one of these personally fabricated parties, with my child choosing their favorite people as the guest list and favorite foods as the party menu, that I formed a burden for how humans hurt humans by showing partiality.

I say all it takes is a group of similar-aged children at a kid's birthday party to trigger everyone's insecurities. The table was spread with decorated cake, lit candles as the centerpiece, color-themed paper products, and balloons. I set out steaming serving trays of my son's favorite meal and invited him and his young friends to come and have a seat. One of his friends loudly announced that he wanted to sit beside a certain other boy. I cringed as I realized how this would sound like instant rejection to all the other guests.

I would learn in those days that we can't and don't need to shield and rescue our children from the many forms of rejection they will face in life. I learned when it came to having friends over, in the days before some children can act and speak unselfishly when put with peers, that "three is a crowd" and one friend at a time can be the less stressful option. I used to make birthday parties where we invited everyone the child's age in our little community and church. I would probably do things differently now that I have watched how much stress this can put on all these young ones comparing themselves. When one child is viewed as the best looking, coolest, smartest, or most talented, it is hard for children not to idolize them and go to great lengths of flattery or bribes to win their approval, hurting many in the path.

Respecter of persons. Favorites. Prejudice. However you want to label it, this is an age-old human problem addressed in James 2:1–9: "But if ye have respect to persons, ye commit sin" (KJV).

What does this have to do with this date and discovering what your child's life message may be? How your child has been treated by others affects them, but with your help, it does not need to define them. God can use these moments to equip your child as they enter their future role in society.

What Can I Do?

1. After your child returns from an event, privately ask specific questions like, "How was tonight for you?" and "Could you enjoy yourself?" and "Did anything difficult happen?"

2. You can play offense in their life by walking with them. Simply ask how it made them feel and validate the negative emotion without casting blame on the other parties since you only heard one side of the story.

3. You can make them feel understood and cared for while encouraging them against harboring thoughts of accusation or self-pity.

4. As you parent, remember the goal is for your child to hear and believe who God made them to be, whether or not others believe in them or treat them well.

5. I tried to remind my children that it is always better to be the one rejected than to be the one through whom rejection is coming according to Scripture. Jesus said, "Blessed are the meek for they shall inherit the earth" (Matt. 5:5, KJV), and "It is impossible that no offenses should come, but woe to him through whom they do come!" (Luke 17:1, KJV).

6. We want to be cautious to not swing that pendulum too far and create a self-righteous attitude or victim mentality in our children. It is healthy to remind them, and ourselves, that we often hear and interpret people's actions and words through filters of ours that they never intended.

I rejoice to tell you that my child who faced a fair share of rejection during that stage exemplifies how God uses hardships to create a life message. This adult now has such a tender, kind, caring, and affirming heart toward all ages, cultures, and social statuses. I delight as I watch how notice is taken of a newcomer at an event or the ones standing alone. These days that child will be found putting uncomfortable or new people at ease with a warm welcome. This child has no enemies and listens patiently to the elderly, the young, and people that are not socially skilled or are insensitive to your timetable.

Your Child's Story

Think about your child's life tests right now or trials and hardships and consider that good character can come out the other side of these tests. You can walk with them, using your experience and wisdom to mentor and encourage them through it!

Most successful people when asked when they started pondering their goals, job, or life mission will share a hardship or childhood experience. Sometimes they share a quote or saying they read or heard in their childhood between the ages of eight and eighteen that impacted them. This tender age is open to resolving their hearts to work toward a noble cause or goal through experiences God brings their way, even beyond our control.

Influences

The positive part is that we as parents have some control and influence of what our children listen to, read, watch, and take in. Our children are like blank hard drives, and we have been given the responsibility and privilege to fill and protect them. When my husband and I responded to God's call, our knowledge was very limited as to how our "yes" might look because of our small worldview. Through our elementary and teen years, we filled our minds with mostly shallow and worldly input through our choice of music, movies, and books.

Instead, we wanted to fill our own children's childhood with access to rich resources. We read current stories from Voice of the Martyrs newsletters and interceded together for the specific people and countries named. We tried to invest in valiant, true stories for their entertainment and have these kinds of films available as an evening or weekend reward for earned screen time.

I borrowed old classic films from the library, like *The Sound of Music*, *Black Beauty*, The Roots series, *Remember the Titans*, and *The Newsies* as well as reenactments of the lives of Abraham Lincoln, Beethoven, and Daniel Boone. We watched movies about great people of faith from Corrie ten Boom to Jim Elliot.

We studied the presidents, and I had our daughters study their wives in high school. We were intrigued by the difference each wife's personality and attitude made in each president's personal success and experience in the White House as well as their contributions to our nation.

For those who are not avid readers and think thick books look daunting, I recommend the Hero Tales series, condensed and compiled by Dave and Neta Jackson. They gave our children an overview of over a hundred faith-filled, influential missionaries and people in the last centuries up to Billy Graham. The whole series make a wonderful read aloud, and they are in a large print for fourth grade level readers to easily read a chapter a day themselves as well. Each attractive hardcover book covers around a dozen notorious Christian lives and includes a few short questions at the end to help the reader remember the key facts shared in the chapter.

We have such a great opportunity to present noble, high

callings and lifestyles before these young minds as the start forming their life message.

I hope on this date:

1. You will get another deeper glimpse into your child's current heart and hear their burdens, goals, and dreams.
2. You can find yourself genuinely interested and excited as you hear your child's thoughts. Enjoy being the trusted one to receive their brain dump.
3. If you do not approve of all their views or goals, you can still be a safe place for them to dream, discuss, and even voice crazy ideas. You can commit your concerns to the Lord in prayer (either with them or in private later if it's stressing you).
4. You can think of your own goals at this age. Haven't we all come a long way since then?!

Your Own Heart Care

1. Allow God's spotlight to shine into your own heart and surrender to God any goals and dreams you hoped your children would have if their goals do not currently match yours.
2. Check to make sure your goals for the child are not derived from your own personal gain or what you never got to do.
3. If you feel God has placed faith in your heart for something specific for this child, by all means, speak it to them in faith! God honors when we speak what we heard from Him out loud in faith.

Date Questions

Offense Check: Is there anything in your heart that I do, have done, or have not done in the past that irritated, belittled, hurt, shamed, angered, or let you down that might hinder you from trusting me and opening up on our date today?

1. What's one of your favorite quotes and songs you've heard lately?

2. When you think about what is going on in our world today, what burdens you the most?

3. Is there a specific people group, continent, or culture that you have thought about going to and making a difference in?

4. If someone gave you $10,000 to help people, what would you do with it?

5. Which of these would click most with you? To help, teach, and encourage young children, poor people, unbelievers, inmates, abused children, orphans, elderly people, or sick people, and how would you envision doing it?

6. If someone is going through a difficult time, would you rather talk with them, read to them, teach them, sing for them, give them presents, help at their house, or pray with them?

7. What change would you like to see in this world? How can you begin to be that change already?

8. If you could give your president, senator, governor, or mayor some advice for how to lead our country and community, what would you say?

9. What would you want the next generations to remember you for?

10. What's the biggest compliment you ever got or could get?

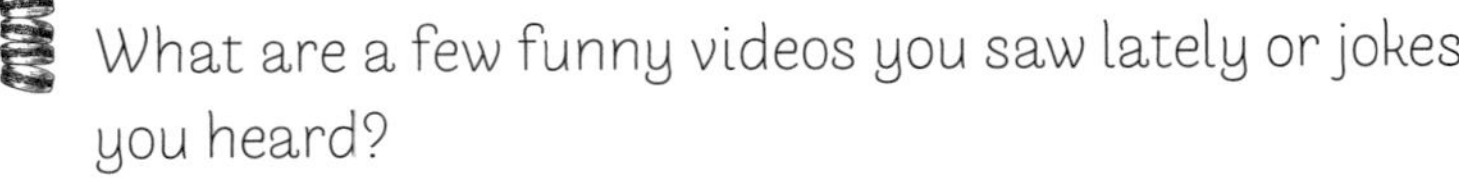 What are a few funny videos you saw lately or jokes you heard?

Closing Question

Now it's your turn if you want to ask me any questions.

Spoken Blessing

I pray God will continue to help you transform any hardships, shameful moments, or other regrets into testimony and passion to help others through similar trials, turning them into a powerful message and blessing to many.

Schedule

Take time to look at your next month's schedule, discuss with your child the next possible date, and pencil it in the index calendar as well as your planner or phone calendar.

Responses to Remember

Date 9:
Recognizing Lies

Parent Tip

The young girl snuggled in the couch corner in her pajamas, tightening her grip on the pillow as she awaited her father's response. She had spilled all her stress and confusion out onto him and was left with a creased forehead peeking out from below the puff of a messy bun. Her father inwardly sighed as an almost righteous anger rose up inside him toward the enemy for causing such havoc in this young girl's heart and mind.

This scene recurred frequently from childhood into teen years for our daughter. She seemed to have an extra sensitive conscience toward God and needed assistance to discern what was the Holy Spirit's promptings and what was false guilt piled onto an innocent victim. This usually happened after talking with friends or wanting a clear conscience before going to bed.

In this same time frame, she heard a testimony of a young girl who had lost her brother and encouraged the whole class to make sure they treat their siblings with kindness and respect while they have them. On top of being very honorable to all of us, it was not unusual for her to go around to most of us family members apologizing for any attitudes she may have projected onto any of us before retiring for the day.

A few things that helped us coach her through those confusing, anxious times were as follows:

1. We are justified by Jesus's sacrifice and righteousness at salvation and don't lose it at very failure or besetting sin.

2. All Christians will be in the sanctification process from salvation on as the Holy Spirit brings things to our attention to confess and repent from. He tells us so we can respond and be reconciled, not for the purpose of keeping us in condemnation.

3. If it is God's voice, He usually reveals our impure motives to repent from more than specific actions or words that came from that motive. If it's the enemy or unnecessary mental clutter, it's usually not clear what to repent from but feelings of confusing accusations, despair, or discouragement.

If you look back at your own deepest hurts, were they not when you had a pure motive but you were misjudged or misunderstood? Words said in those moments pierce right into your heart.

God may be the most sensitive, softhearted Being there is.

Isn't that a mind-blasting thought? He is the hugest, strongest, smartest, most talented, most influential, most mature, most experienced, longest living, perfect, authoritative, revered Being. And could He be the most easily hurt?

If we are hurt in areas we are pure and innocent, isn't

that a part of what holiness is? Is not holiness total purity, void of any ounce of wrong motive or unloving or selfish intent?

If that is the state of the heart of the Father, His Son, and the Holy Spirit in us at all times, how often is He hurt or dishonored by man—by me? He understands the pain of being misunderstood.

Personal Reflections

Before the Date

As your child opens their heart, watch for wetting eyes, downcast face, and even deep weeping as your child might relive some of these moments in life where they were very misunderstood by other humans and it cut deep. Prepare yourself to be comfortable with emotional pain, crying, and even anger or increased volume if they start unwrapping wounds in front of you. Be very kind and gentle. Hold your child and give plenty of time to process any hard things they are willing to talk about.

Ask them what the phrase or word for the emotion is that they felt and what they have believed about themselves or others since that event. There is a list of negative emotions in the index that they can look at to help put into words what they are feeling or had felt. You can also go to the Heart Care part of the index for further guidance.

Date Questions

Offense Check: Is there anything in your heart that I do, have done, or have not done in the past that irritated, belittled, hurt, shamed, angered, or let you down that might hinder you from trusting me and opening up on our date today?

☲ What is the most exciting thing you were a part of in the last year?

1. What was the worst thing anyone has said to you or about you, and how have you viewed yourself since then?

2. Were there other things that were said that you have hard time forgetting during or since that time period?

3. Parent: Ask them to expound on why and when if they can.

4. Did any teachers or authorities ever make you feel inferior or not good enough?

5. Have you felt mostly welcomed, wanted, and loved by us? (Or by those who brought you up?)

6. What words that us parents have said have affected whether you feel accepted or like you weren't good enough?

7. What have you sensed or felt from friends that made you feel unwelcome or unwanted in a group?

8. Has anything happened among church people or employees that wasn't upbuilding to you?

9. What is the very earliest memory you have, good or hard, and where did it occur?

☲ Who's your favorite comedian, and what is a funny line you can quote of theirs?

10. How do you think the opposite gender in your age group tends to view or perceive you?

11. How do you think God the Father views you as He watches you day by day, and how do you picture Jesus's involvement in your life nowadays?

Would you rather jump into a pool of gummy worms, Skittles, Reese's Pieces, Oreo pudding, or bubble tea?

Closing Question

Now it's your turn if you want to ask me any questions.

Spoken Blessing

Ask them to bring to the Father any negative thoughts or phrases they battle with about themselves and confess receiving that condemnation as truth, asking Jesus to take back the ground in their heart given to the enemy and cleanse them with His blood. Follow it by praying that the Lord would show them where they first believed the lie and accusation and bring revelation or opposing Scripture and truth to their hearts and help them have victory by recognizing it in the future when they think it.

Schedule

Take time to look at your next month's schedule, discuss with your child the next possible date, and pencil it in the index calendar as well as your planner or phone calendar.

Responses to Remember

Your Body

Parent Tip

Does your preteen slam doors, yell, or cry more quickly these days? Fret not, their hormones are raging. Your little girl suddenly feels like a woman who is experiencing PMS, and she has a harder time dealing with hard emotions because of her body's physical demands.

This is one of the hardest stages for your child. On top of their body changing both mentally and emotionally, questions of personal identity are rising in their minds. This comes from the battle between questions forming in their mind: Will my friends think well of me and accept me? What do my parents actually stand for? What do I believe for myself? Middle schoolers need trusted adults who remain in tune with them and their relationship changes. Weekly support, understanding, and affirmation from those adults has never been more crucial.

Your child is becoming more keenly aware of their own human anatomy, and they need your help to navigate as it changes into an adult body. A parent who plays good offense will want to be the first, not the last, to inform their child of what to expect when their body transitions. When these details are talked about freely as something good and God-ordained, you can open a door to learning about their bodies in a pure, positive manner.

Our Story

When our children were getting to the age that they might either be exposed to the facts of life by peers or experience puberty soon themselves, we watched a video I had purchased with explanations from a Christian nurse and her son. I planned a time alone with the child, watched the video, and then opened up for questions.

For our oldest, I had baked a batch of buttermilk cookies and decided that icing them together while we watched might make it less awkward. My husband had taken the four younger ones so it could be an intentional time discussing the science of birds and bees. My husband then planned a trip to a neighboring state to buy our first four-wheeler for this oldest son's birthday gift, using that as his time to discuss some man-to-man matters about things like erection and masturbation and to answer any questions he had.

Our oldest daughter loved to make everything into a ceremony, so I booked a room in a local city hotel for the two of us and invited her friends to have a party and swim there earlier in the day. I showed her the video that evening when she and I were snuggled together in the privacy of our hotel room and afterward gave her as much time as she wanted for discussion and questions.

With each child, I think we introduced the subject a year earlier than the last, knowing that information was all around them. We wanted to be the ones introducing the appropriate terminology and view of body parts and body functions to our child, teaching Bible-based reproduction.

With our oldest children, we started the subject around eleven or twelve, and by the youngest we shared by age eight or nine.

Before the Date

My husband and I have taken the approach: how vulnerable you are with your children is how vulnerable they will be with you. We confessed to them where we had failed morally and some of the consequences that came with that even though we have lived in victory since we were born again and made Jesus our Lord. We named and renounced all the iniquities we were aware of in our lives and our forefathers. If someone in our family has opened a door for the enemy, we can close it in Jesus's name to avoid the iniquities to be passed down to the third and fourth generation, halting them for the next generation because of Jesus's precious blood shed for us.

We tell our children a lot of the mistakes we made in the hopes that they don't need to repeat them. Thankfully, they are choosing better paths and are much more mature in Christ than we were at their ages. Believe in God being with and guiding your child! He can do more than we can, even when we are present with them.

As you approach this subject, relax. Take a deep breath. Act normal. One of our sons says, "It's only as awkward as you make it." You have the privilege to talk about this with your child.

To prepare you for the first question on this date, you want to know the meaning of your child's name. If you don't know what their name means, Google it and give your own interpretation of what you hope that means for their life.

Personal Reflections

Date Questions

Offense Check: Is there anything in your heart that I do, have done, or have not done in the past that irritated, belittled, hurt, shamed, angered, or let you down that might hinder you from trusting me and opening up on our date today?

1. Do you like your name? Explain. (Tell them why you chose the name if you know.)

2. Do you know any events that your mother attended or world events that were happening while she was pregnant with you?

   Parent: If you can, Google highlights of world and national monumental or memorable events that occurred the year they were born.

3. What do you find as pros and cons about being your gender?

   What is something that is hard for you to understand about the opposite gender and why they act or think the way they do?

4. As you recognize you are physically maturing and experiencing changes in your body to become an adult, is there anything you are not yet comfortable with or still adjusting to? How is it affecting you?

5. Have you heard of or experienced wet dreams?

   Parent: Explain that it is nature's way of releasing the semen their body is now producing, and they need not feel ashamed of it. (Further discussed in the QR code video.)

What is a favorite vacation, field trip, or holiday memory you have from your childhood?

6. Has there been a discussion or activity among your friends concerning girls' periods or masturbation? Do you understand a female's cycle and how many days out of the month she can conceive or have a baby start growing in her womb?

   Parent: Share your own childhood experiences, positive and negative, to encourage trust between you two on this subject for life.

7. God has beautifully made our bodies male and female for a good purpose. I want you to never feel like it is an uncomfortable or inappropriate subject. Our Holy God said it was a good thing when He created the first humans. All children are curious about our different bodies and how they change as we mature. You are probably noticing changes in your own body as you mature into a young (man or woman).

8. Have you or someone else exposed you to pictures or videos of naked people, and if so, how was that experience for you?

9. We as parents want to walk with you on this learning journey as you grow up.

10. Have you or someone else attempted to show their private parts, causing you or someone else to be uncomfortable?

11. Explain to me how you currently view the subject of girls who dress revealing their womanly shape and a lot of skin or covering it more for modesty's sake? How is this affecting you and your friends right now?

12. What are some of your personal thoughts and goals in courtship relationships, and how do you feel about becoming a parent in the future?

 What is your favorite feature or ride in an amusement park?

Closing Question

Now it's your turn if you want to ask me any questions.

Spoken Blessing

Pray over your child for power from God to walk in victory and honest accountability with a trusted Christian, older mentor, friend, or you.

God protects and cares for whatever is dedicated to Him for His dominion in this Life. Have you or would you be ready to dedicate your body to Jesus since He paid dearly with His blood to redeem it and your soul and spirit back from darkness to the kingdom of light and His glory while you are on earth?

Schedule

Congratulations! If you took the dates in order, you have now completed all the subjects we offer for this age level! If you have not completed all the earlier dates for this age level, you can continue having them in the order and pace you prefer.

Responses to Remember

Responses to Remember

HIGH SCHOOL

AGES 15–17

POSITION OF ADULT ROLE:

House rules can transition to goals and guidelines that you bless. The hope is that this budding adult starts to choose better options rather than being forced and feeling like a controlled child. When you feel troubled about something in your teen's life, ask more questions. It is time to transition into the role of a sensitive listener, sympathizer, discerning protector, and life adviser rather than a fearful, hovering, dominating, or ever-nagging force.

Assume the best of your child and build on trust and honesty instead of distrust and deceit. Like our nation's judicial system, in order to accomplish the Golden Rule in how we view and treat people, we assume our children are innocent until proven guilty.

Creating a Safe Place

I arose from the mocha wicker chair on the deck to move inside and fill my empty glass with another flavor to infuse my next eight ounces of water. As my eyes adjusted from the outdoor deck sunshine to the cozy, shaded lighting of our dine-in kitchen, I observed a tall figure hunched over a sizzling pan creating his own personalized cuisine for lunch. (This is a luxury you parents of busy school students can teach and look forward to if you don't have your teenagers enjoying making their own meals yet.) As I clattered my glass full of fresh ice, I decided to make use of his appearance in my "pondering zone" and crafted a specific but casual question for him.

I was thinking back to some of the scenarios my husband and I have faced during our children's teen years where we felt compelled to confront one of our children about a subject, habit, or behavior. Rather than assuming we did a good job, I wondered how this grown child would rate the approaches we have taken in those times.

A huge part of creating a safe culture where our children will open up and be vulnerable is to keep living that way, in vulnerability with them, in every stage of life. My questions to him were: what have we as parents done to shut him down? And what advice would he have for parents on how to approach a child about something in their life?

Creating a Culture

As parents our responses can be defining moments. Perhaps we see or sense something in one of our children's lives that causes us to fear or think negatively about their personal well-being. Sometimes we jump to conclusions about their current character or moral status.

After hearing my son's thoughts and returning to my desk, I asked myself these questions: have I ever come across something questionable in one of my children's lives or personal belongings that made me want to panic and be very disheartened in their future? Yes and yes. Was the child not as deep in sin as I thought and it turned out to be okay? Yes and yes again! Did I confront the child in my emotional state with judgment? That varies, yes and no.

Have there been various outcomes of hurt feelings, shutdown, and misunderstanding versus peaceful surrender, honesty, and reconciliation? For sure. Have I handled confrontation in the wrong way? Absolutely. Humble apologies and amends were needed in order for the child to open up and trust me again. "A soft answer turneth away wrath" (Proverbs 15:1, KJV) is one of the simplest, most practical principles God gave us that works every time!

A few things to consider when we discern if something is amiss in our child's life.

How will I view this subject from my past experiences?

1. From a perspective of failure? Since I gave into the flesh in this area, am I expecting my child's motives to be as impure or intentional as my own were?

2. From a perspective of abstinence and victory when I was tempted?
3. Or perhaps I was never tempted in this area, and I feel more righteous than my child?

My husband and I experienced our adolescence and teen years without having made a confession of Christ as our Savior or Lord. Neither of us were transparent with our parents in those years. Therefore, our habits, goals, and values all reflected our selfish nature. After repenting and renouncing all of it and asking Jesus to be our Lord, all of that changed dramatically.

Still, we were left with a lot of associations from our personal experiences, and we were quick to assume that a physical thing signified a specific motive. For example, we made quick jumps to assume that liking cool cars meant idolatry, softball could lead to partying, or certain clothing and hairstyles were associated with sensuality, rebellion, or pride. We associated specific music styles with specific positions of the heart, any alcoholic content with drunkenness, theaters with violence and immorality, playing cards with gambling. Our natural response viewed moms as mostly domestic and dads as more authoritarian than relational. Even specific terminology or words may bring a picture or double meaning to our minds.

As parents we do well to recognize how we have formed filters of thinking through our own experiences or people we know. God has given my husband much wisdom from his much asking, as James 1:5 tells us. When we hear or discover something about our adolescent and adult children that is disappointing or even alarming, often his response is, "Let's hear the person out and see where they are coming from before we conclude or pass judgment." Isn't that how we all want to be treated?

We have come to try to follow these basic steps in a loving confrontation. More details are available in the index under "Kind Confrontations."

1. Once you are calm and have prayed about it, ask the child when they would have a few minutes to discuss something. Decide on the time and room in the house (unless that feels like it's making it too big a deal for the child and might actually add unnecessary fear or anxiety). We try not to let it drag overnight into the next day for the child's sake of wondering and worrying, possibly making it a bigger deal than it needs to be.

2. You can start the meeting with humor or light talk but then go into reassuring them that your goal as parents is to walk with, support, protect, guide but also release and trust them throughout their different seasons of life. This meeting is because you want to walk through all of life's good and hard stuff.

3. We usually try to express some good things we see and appreciate in their life currently and then state that we have a few questions to ask them about a concern for their well-being.

4. We then proceed with sharing what information we were given or came upon that caused our concern and remind them that we came to them for the truth and the whole story, instead of going by other sources. We welcome our child to give their viewpoint and input on what actually happened.

Date Questions

1. What was the highlight of your last six months?

2. What has been your biggest trial lately?

3. Who do you tend to talk to when you are going through something hard, and what is it about them that makes you feel comfortable with them?

4. Are there things I do or have done that tend to cause you to put up a wall between us?

5. What are some areas you don't feel like I am hearing and understanding you in?

6. Is there something we as parents promised that we never carried out?

7. Our goal is to be your protectors. Has there been a time that you did not feel protected by us?

8. Is there anything that happened in your childhood that seems to still be affecting you today?

9. What is something I could do throughout the week to encourage you?

10. Where and when is your favorite place and time to get alone, away from people?

Would you rather zip-line into a pool of whipped cream, cappuccino, Nutella, donut holes, popcorn, or Skittles?

Closing Question:

And now I'd like to give you the opportunity to ask me any questions you have.

Spoken Blessing to Child

Reconcile by asking humbly for their forgiveness for specific things the child mentioned. This includes anything that shut them down, even if your motives were pure and you had no idea.

Thank you so much for giving your time to share honestly and discuss these things. We as parents want to walk beside you in the fun, exciting, and hard as you are growing into a fine adult we are and will be proud of. I see you becoming more _______________, and you seem to be more aware of _______________ and able to _______________ without anyone telling you to. I am glad you have _______________ as a friend when you need to talk. I always think you look nice in that _______________ (shirt, outfit, haircut).

Please feel free to bring stuff on your heart to me even if I get busy and forget to ask. Just ask me if I have a minute and I know you want to tell me something that is on your mind. I need you to help me become a better parent by communicating clearly and kindly as we learn from each other and give grace when we both face new stuff.

Ask the young adult if they would want to end the date by praying and committing the things you discussed to God.

Sample of Child's Closing Prayer: Heavenly Father, you know both me and my (mom or dad, grandparent, or mentor) and see how we have at times hurt and misunderstood each other without trying. Can you please help me to forgive when (he or she) said _______________ and _______________ and did not realize how it made me feel so _______________ and

Testimony Video

_______________ at the time. I realize now how unaware (he or she) was, and I want to extend grace because You did to me on the cross while I was yet a sinner. Please, Lord, take back the ground and close the door to the enemy I had opened through bitterness and anger and replace it with love and mercy from Your Spirit. In Jesus's name, Amen.

Sample of Parent's Closing Prayer: Lord, please forgive me where I shut down _______________ (child's name) by _______________ and _______________. Help me to be more sensitive and discerning of (his or her) feelings and thoughts.

Optional question to ask: Do you have preference on which of us parents you'd prefer with which subjects on the upcoming dates?

Schedule

Take time to look at your next month's schedule, discuss with your child the next possible date, and pencil it in the index calendar as well as your planner or phone calendar.

Responses to Remember

Routines and Relationships

Parent Tip

What might be some reasons children rebel? The Old Testament has some hard but interesting tips we can glean from other people's mistakes. We can read and observe how Eli the priest did not correct or restrain his sons for transgressions that he knew they were committing. I Samuel 3:13 states: "For I have told him that I will judge him forever for the iniquity which he knows, because his sons made themselves vile, and he did not restrain them" (KJV).

I Samuel 8:3 simply says, "His sons walked not in his ways" (KJV). We all can study Samuel's life and ask God for revelation as to why this was. Good parents can have resistant children. In the New Testament we read, "Fathers, provoke not to wrath . . . lest they be discouraged" (Eph. 6:4, KJV) and "God resists the proud but gives grace to the humble" (James 4:6, NKJV). In the Old Testament we read, "pride goeth before . . . a fall" (Prov. 16:18, KJV) and "Iniquity . . . to the third and fourth generation" (Num. 14:18, ESV).

A few observations my husband and I have made are that selfish parenting equals selfish children who will not have their parents as a priority when they are older. Rules without relationship reap rebellion. "You reap what you sow" can be very detrimental or rewarding depending on what we were planting. Priorities are caught rather than taught. Is your reputation more important? It's wise for us to do inventory. Have we dishonored, belittled, and scolded our children in front of other people to make ourselves look good and solve the problem? They will do the same back when they are adults, unless they choose to show mercy toward your offenses or secret sin. We have found that children from ages two to one hundred are mostly very forgiving if parents of any stage of life will only acknowledge where and how they have wronged them.

Your Own Heart Care

Has one of your parents or authorities ever said or done something hurtful and went on living peacefully while you couldn't believe they never apologized? I had a quote like that in my head for over a decade. When I thought of burying that parent, I realized it might need to be my move to have this cleared from my conscience. I remember as a young Christian recalling someone asking, "Whose job is it to go first in clearing up an offense?" The wise teacher responded, "The one who is most concerned about their own spiritual state will go first."

This applies to all other relationships in our lives as well. After applying this in one scenario, I found the specific person I often felt most uncomfortable with in a group is now the one I feel the most understood and appreciated by. I shared in private with that person how I had perceived a certain comment from them. The person had not remembered saying it as I took it and clarified how they felt and how they had intended the comment differently. All those months of struggling vanished in one simple confession of humility.

The above conversation was local, but my parents live out of state. We only saw each other a few times a year and often in group settings. Timing and being led by the Spirit in sharing "the offense" in humility and honor depended greatly on the outcome of these conversations that could potentially feel confrontational to them.

In my case, I felt I needed to plan a specific trip home by myself while my husband was occupied with ministry elsewhere. Upon my arrival at my parents' home, I put an Amen on my last hours of prayer that filled my trip there. I took a few deep breaths as I mounted the familiar porch steps to the front door. Is, or has, my relationship been relaxed with this parent to talk heart-to-heart things? No. Have I done this prayerfully with my parents many times before anyway? Yes.

Both the attitude and atmosphere for these discussions seem to assist its potential for a peaceful, thorough, and positive outcome. So after some small talk catching up over a meal, I asked if we could go to their front yard and sit by the pond to have a discussion about something. They gladly agreed and placed three lawn chairs in the woods clearing by the water's edge where our low voices mingled with croaking frogs, buzzing insects, and chirping birds in the summer night. I remember telling them there are a few things that had hurt me, and I just wanted to share them with them even though I had already tried to forgive them many years ago.

I described the scenes to see if they would recall. To my surprise, the person did not even recall what had been said at all. I couldn't believe I had taken it as such a personal dagger to my heart when they didn't remember their motive, much less saying any of it! After the relief and healing ointment of their kind response of regret and sorrow for hurting me, I felt a keen sense of foolishness for waiting to have it clarified for so many years. I will never forget the personal freedom gained between my parents and me on that teary, moonlit night accomplishing that Fourth of July journey home for peace. I want to do what it takes to say I have attempted to live in peace with everyone, for this is a beautiful and valuable legacy we have experienced in my husband's family and desire to pass on to the next generation.

"If it be possible, as much as lieth in you, live peaceably with all men" (Rom. 12:18, KJV).

"Follow peace with all men, and holiness without which, no man shall see the Lord" (Hebrews 12:14, KJV).

I experienced a huge peace and laughing release by voicing my heart with both my local friend and my parents, and leaving those conversations felt amazingly refreshing.

Date Questions

Offense Check: Is there anything in your heart that I do, have done, or have not done in the past that irritated, belittled, hurt, shamed, angered, or let you down that might hinder you from trusting me and opening up on our date today?

1. Who do you feel "gets you" or seems to understand and hear you the most in our family?

2. Is there currently someone in your life that you are getting to know and hope to pursue a deeper connection with?

3. Is there a specific challenge right now for you to get along with someone in our home?

4. Are there some changes that could be made in our home for it to be more enjoyable?

5. What is something we as parents could do to help set a better culture for connection and unity in our home?

6. Are you aware of any circumstances that broke the trust between anyone in our home?

7. What's something we could do together that would be fun or exciting to you?

8. Do you have any suggestions on how we as parents can be more involved in any certain area or interest in your life?

9. Do you consider our delegation of home upkeep and daily jobs a sufficient and fair one?

10. Is there someone in our family you may need to consider making peace with or forgive? (Matthew 18)

 Would you rather live in a jungle tree house, the top floor suite of a skyscraper, a boathouse, a van, a glass house in the mountains, or on a western ranch?

Closing Question

And now I'd like to give you the opportunity to ask me any questions you have.

Spoken Blessings

Lord, I thank you for bringing (name of child) _________ into our lives and for this precious date time together for just the two of us. I thank you for the opportunity (name of child) ________ has to influence brothers and sisters, relatives, neighbors, school and community youth and children. I pray you will continue to give (him or her) compassion to those who might be older in years, less fortunate, struggling in health or mobility, or slower learners and know how (he or she) can be an encouragement and a loving, safe place for them. I pray faith onto (name of child) ______, and I pray for a wise yet humble and discerning heart as (he or she) tries to take the high road and set an example for others. Thank you, Lord, for giving us health, a home, and your protection. In Jesus's strong Name, Amen.

Schedule

Take time to look at your next month's schedule, discuss with your child the next possible date, and pencil it in the index calendar as well as your planner or phone calendar.

Responses to Remember

Maintaining a
Clear Conscience

Parent Tip

Do you believe supporting your children emotionally and spiritually is as much your calling as providing for their physical needs? There have been times I catch myself responding to our children's struggles as a bother distracting me from all the other hats I am wearing. These are the moments I have overlooked both the honor and weight of preparing a soul for a lifetime and eternity. We can so innocently dedicate our children for God's purpose as babies only to neglect our stewardship of them along the way.

As I read about King David in II Samuel 12, 13, and 16, I am painfully reminded of our own stewardship battle between time spent with our children and broader callings. When new opportunities, promotions, and leadership roles come around, I watch how the most influential Godly man in the land of Israel, endowed with many handsome sons and beautiful daughters of influence, seemed to lack time and energy to mentor, protect, and lead his children.

When Amnon pretended to be sick, why did David not discern his son Amnon's hypocrisy and lies? Was he too busy and preoccupied? He could have protected Tamar from this ridiculous request to make cakes in Amnon's chamber, which ended in his lovely daughter never being able to marry a worthy man.

When Amnon sinned against her, it was the beginning of a sad fulfillment. Through the prophet Nathan, God had foretold that David's next generations would reap immorality and violence because of his murder of Uriah and adultery with Bathsheba. When the news of Tamar comes to the throne, David's response is wrath. Why? His own guilt? David could have had a family meeting and openly acknowledged his own immoral sin to his children. He could have taken responsibility to justly punish Amnon and personally comfort Tamar.

Instead, Tamar's drop-dead-gorgeous, raven-haired, blemishless-physiqued brother Absalom invited her to live with him. After watching his beautiful, scarred sister's desolation every day, he took serious offense for her, forming strong hate for the perpetrator and stoking the desire for revenge.

Just two years later, Absalom acted by arranging the murder of his half brother Amnon, which led to fleeing into isolation from his dad for three years. Eventually, David's trusty army general, Joab, intervened. Although allowed to move back home, Absalom remained uninvited into the presence of his father and was given the cold shoulder of silent treatment as punishment for the murder. After two unbearable years and attempts to appeal to Joab, Absalom set Joab's barley field on fire to finally get his attention.

Absalom's desperate desire to see and greet his dad, even if he had to die to do so, finally came to pass. In that same throne room, the king had been wroth at the rape of

Tamar and later tore his clothes and wept for Amnon. Now, the father laid eyes on and kissed his five-years-yearned-for son. The results of five years of rejection and David's absence in his son's life and hardships resulted in distrust replacing loyalty.

Entrenched identity lies in Absalom's heart led to the stealing of Israel's hearts and devising a rebellion that ultimately took the throne by force. This culminated in the death of 20,000 Israelites. And finally, to end the tale, Absalom was caught and hung by his beautiful hair to be slain by none other than his barley-growing neighbor and longtime advocate Joab and his men.

I always choke up and feel the pangs of a parents' deepest loss as I picture the next scene. Through the city gate falls the out-of-breath Cushi bearing tidings of victory! He spills out what he thinks will be the best news ever told: the death of all the enemies, especially the ringleader, Absalom! David's throne has been reclaimed!

Knowing David is not like most kings, I hold my breath for his response and read, as he realizes Absalom's life was not spared, "And the king was much moved, and went up to the chamber over the gate, and wept" (2 Sam. 18:33, KJV). You talk about a parent who had so many emotions of regret and love! It seems as though he wished he had died in his son's stead.

Imagine Joab's viewpoint by now. Here is an army general that must have been just about fed up with doing the dirty job of a king's love life, children's rebellions, and sin issues! From having an innocent Uriah killed, sending a widow with a story to get the "pretty boy" son back home, to having his barley burned so the king would finally acknowledge his son. Next the still unhappy pretty boy's plan evolved to take the throne. Joab now gets in on the job of helping the whole king's huge household minus ten concubines, a counselor, and a priest, literally move out and flee Judah. He is put in charge of thousands for David against thousands of Israelite kinsmen whose hearts had been won by the cunning young Absalom conversing daily at the city gate.

Is a rich but lonely son craving validation and identity to be spoken by his father for years bad enough to have his own dad killed for it? Joab had his "bloody man" faults, but he sure has my respect for his personal loyalty to David and being there and carrying out so much dirty work for David's personal goals and family problems, spoken and unspoken.

May you have God's divine discernment as you listen to the heart of your child. Listen for what is clouding their mind from being confident and clear as they face people and look into their eyes. You'd rather have some bad news now while you are still in their lives and they are in your home.

Your Story

Here is time to reflect on your own moral state during your teen years. Consider what a different set of temptations your child is facing in this current culture. If you have been immoral in the past and have never shared with your child how you opened the door to the enemy back then and how you dealt with the temptations since then, I urge you to share it now. The gender of the child should make no difference other than discerning how specific to make your confession. Coming clean and opening up honestly will build trust and bring down walls. If you want honesty and transparency in your home with your children, you need to show the way. If you haven't been living this way, you can expect it to take some time for them not to feel like you have a manipulative agenda for doing so now.

When we hide our sins from our children, we may find ourselves in repeated immoral messes in the next genera-

tion such as in II Samuel 12, 13, and 16. We as parents are responsible to protect our children and help them find victory in temptations as much as is in our power.

Another concept illustrated here is "bad company corrupts good manners." This is hard to avoid when they are cousins, like David's nephew Shimei's advice to Amnon.

Personal Reflections

Date Questions

Offense Check: Is there anything in your heart that I do, have done, or have not done in the past that irritated, belittled, hurt, shamed, angered, or let you down that might hinder you from trusting me and opening up on our date today?

 What's your favorite music album right now?

1. What is your friend groups' take or experience on the subjects of smoking, vaping, any amount of alcohol intake, or form of drugs? Have you been offered or tried any forms of these? And how was your experience?

2. Have we ever told you how each of us parents were first exposed to any of this and what our experience was?

3. Is there someone of the opposite gender you've been communicating with, and would you be comfortable expounding a bit on the depth of that relationship?

4. What is one of your main concerns or fears that you are dealing with currently?

5. Is there a memory or circumstance that is hard for you not to feel resentful about?

6. When was the last time you reacted to someone, and what words or actions triggered your emotions?

7. Has anyone exposed or introduced you to something questionable or inappropriate in the past or lately?

8. Have you been battling temptation with viewing any type of inappropriate content?

9. Do you have peace about all your messaging interactions with friends?

10. Has anything happened, in the past or lately, that hinders you from feeling pure and having a clear conscience?

🥤 Who is a favorite book or movie character that inspires or amuses you?

🥤 What is your go-to order at a coffee shop?

Closing Question

And now I'd like to give you the opportunity to ask me any questions you have.

Spoken Blessing

Thank your teenager for their openness and honesty and offer if they feel comfortable for your adult child to verbally release to God anything that has been on their conscience.

Sample Child's Prayer: Lord, please forgive me for not being sensitive to _____________ and for _____________ and _____________. Please cleanse my heart and mind from _____________ with the precious blood you shed for me and all my sin. I renounce the area of _____________ that I opened a door to the enemy and pray you will take residence as Lord in that area instead.

Encourage them to make anything right with any people that they have wronged or dishonored. Speak kindly, thanking them for trusting you with their innermost thoughts. Pray a blessing on their broken and contrite heart and honesty.

Sample Parent's Prayer: May the Lord Bless you for your honesty. Psalm 51:17 says the preferred sacrifice from us to the Lord is a broken spirit. The psalmist affirms that a broken and contrite heart He, God, will not despise.

Schedule

Take time to look at your next month's schedule, discuss with your child the next possible date, and pencil it in the index calendar as well as your planner or phone calendar.

Responses to Remember

Skills to Steward

Dave: My dad trusted me with his farm equipment and team of Percheron horses at a young age, which helped shape my confidence and trustworthiness as a teenager. We apply this concept when our teens join youth socials, get their license, and have the family credit card in their name for building confidence, trust, and character. They pay their own bills that are agreed upon at the end of the month.

Parent Tip

Rolling into my fiftieth year of life, I had already undergone a biopsy to check for cancer and watched a close friend have her pelvic area butchered in order to remove all of the cancerous tumor with fingers. Praise the Lord with His healing and all her studies and natural efforts, she was cancer free a year later. I told my family and some of my friends that if I would need to say goodbye to this world and transition to my awaited eternal Kingdom, I would consider my life on earth a fully wonderful and complete gift already, lacking no good thing!

God has helped me greatly to live out my goal of living daily "so as to have the least amount of regrets," and He has prospered me to be rich in relationships and experiences. I would want no one to pity me or think I had been cut short.

During the first two decades of their lives, my husband and I lived very openly with our children and spent more time with them than any other humans. Unlike many circuit-riding preachers of old, we were blessed to be a part of an evangelistic ministry that facilitated doing ministry together as a family. We are so grateful to also have lived in an era, and in a country, where homeschooling was acknowledged as a way to educate and train your children for life, and God financially provided all we needed for that lifestyle.

When we have no hidden sin or ongoing unresolved conflict, and we allow the Holy Spirit to cleanse us from selfish motives for our children, I take comfort in the saying "more is caught than taught." One day, you may bring up one of your major burdens and hear your adult children say, *"Oh, Mom, we know how you feel about this, believe us. We think about this all the time if the subject comes up! You have instilled all these principles in us from young on up. We could hardly forget if we tried to."* Isn't that encouraging?! If we spend enough time together and freely talk about what we learn and believe and live it out faithfully, asking for forgiveness when needed, we can just *be*, and they will *become* baby shoots of us. As a parent, relax! Just *be* when you are around your children, and they will know your heart and goals for them.

Personal Reflections

Before the Date

We as parents and mentors should always be working ourselves out of a job. Think in terms of preparing your children for life without you. When you ponder how many normal housekeeping duties to teach or include your sons and daughters in, consider if they would live alone or get married. What skills should both boys and girls know to make better homeowners, roommates, or spouses? Though it takes more time, we attempted to teach both our sons and daughter basic cleaning, cooking, loading a dishwasher, baking bread, yard and vehicle upkeep, plumbing, energy bill saving habits, proper laundry sorting, stain removal and ironing, hospitality etiquette, and returning borrowed items better than received.

I have the sweet privilege of stewarding my mother-in-law's large distressed wooden board found in her canning cellar. It is full of memories where she used to chop up holiday chocolate blocks and roll out her flaky pie crusts. Now it has become my favorite charcuterie board. Our children know how to oil and care for wood and leather as they clean their own wooden instruments, shoes, and car interiors.

What about seasoning and cleaning a cast-iron pan versus stainless steel or a nonstick one, do they know the varying tools needed for each one? Have fun hearing their perspective of skills attained and jobs desired and work with them, always remembering your own state of mind as a teen. Be honest if you didn't help much at home or wish you would have learned more from your parents before you moved out.

Date Questions

Offense Check: Is there anything in your heart that I do, have done, or have not done in the past that irritated, belittled, hurt, shamed, angered, or let you down that might hinder you from trusting me and opening up on our date today?

1. What goals have you accomplished lately that you have been working on?

2. Is there a new job, ministry, or mission you have been pondering?

3. Is there any skill or service you have considered doing for extra income?

4. Have you considered investing time in any of the arts like drama, speaking, voice lessons, music, sketching, journaling, writing, poetry, painting, architectural design, crafting, needlework, confectionery, or macramé?

5. If you had a choice to either repaint and repurpose an old piece of furniture or buy a new one to update your room, which would you choose?

6. If you and I could take a day or weekend trip, what would you want to do or where would you want to go?

7. Do you have any home improvement ideas for our home that would really update it or make a big difference experientially?

8. Is there any home improvement project you would gladly take charge of or help make happen if we did it?

9. If you had time and money to pursue more education and experiences, what field would you be drawn to?

10. What is a position you would be honored to serve in or a committee you would enjoy being on at your school, church, or in our community?

 If you were stranded in a cabin alone with friends for four days, would you rather be blindfolded or have to go without talking, sleeping, or eating the whole time?

Closing Question

And now I'd like to give you the opportunity to ask me any questions you have.

Spoken Blessing

I want to bless you ___________ (name of child) for how you serve our home and family by ___________ and ____________. For how you cooperate and are considerate, honorable, and kind to those you rub shoulders with in school, church, and our greater community. I want to support and take interest in how you are good at and enjoy _________ and are furthering your skill set in the area of ___________. I want to value what is fun and important to you because I care about your happiness and fulfillment in life.

Schedule

Take time to look at your next month's schedule, discuss with your child the next possible date, and pencil it in the index calendar as well as your planner or phone calendar.

Responses to Remember

Date 5:

Discovering Their Personality

The wipers kept a steady swishing rhythm against the pelting rain—unlike my heart, which seemed to have picked up an irregular speed—as we neared my familiar neighborhood. At school, my teacher had threatened to give any class disruptors a personal ride home if they received enough points under their names. Here I sat receiving the very first complimentary ride, stuck in a long line of traffic.

I was curious what she would actually tell my parents when we arrived. From my perspective, I was merely a less shrewd conman when it came to getting away with classmate exchanges. I hadn't meant to deliberately dishonor my authorities.

While my teacher was pondering her own thoughts, the traffic halted suddenly, and we rear-ended the car in front of us, jolting both of us forward into our restraining seat belts. She worriedly checked if I was all right, then released me to walk to my house while she talked to the other driver and an arriving police officer. I nodded and smiled, thinking surely Providence was proving my innocence.

I thought I had dodged a bullet at the time, but I could have used a little instruction on honoring your authorities and respecting guidelines for everyone's sake, in spite of my butterfly, fun, relational personality. It is very wise for us parents to go to any of our children's caretakers, sitters, teachers, youth overseers, and grandparents and ask them about the character and behavior that they observe in our children, positive and negative, when we are not present. This will give us information to improve training up this certain child in the way this child specifically should go.

What I do take comfort in is knowing God can cover for our children where we have fallen short! Here is a perfect illustration of how He did so in my life. As we already know, I had gotten caught disrupting with whispering, notes, and stifling laughter. But I had also followed through with a dare to sneak a piece of bubblegum from the brown scrunched paper bag of occasional student rewards. I snuck into my teacher's long cupboard while she was grading papers at the other end of the room during winter recess. And yes, my clever teacher heard the brown bag rattle and caught me in the act. It feels like the dumbest risk to take for something I don't even really like today, but that was me. Despite some dysfunction, I thank God for my carefree childhood, where new risks were an adventure and leadership came naturally (although it was terrible leadership at times).

The part where God's gentle, redeeming sense of humor came in was after we moved back east from Arizona and bought our first house in a small city in Ohio called Millersburg. After getting my diploma through a GED at age nineteen, I had been converted to Christianity and asked for Jesus's Lordship. Now I was living out my life as a married mother of three. The Lord knew I wanted to clear my conscience from all my past minor and major transgressions against people, and He led us to buy our first little home in the city next to one of them.

Guess who we unknowingly had just moved two houses down from? Yep, my former sixth grade teacher, her husband, and their six children! You can laugh with me when I discovered who our neighbor was and rejoice as I cleared my conscience of the stolen bubble game and violating her boundaries! We ended up sharing homeschooling tips over our backyard fences after I had cleared my conscience to her response of bygone oblivion, followed by her whole frame shaking in laughter.

Before the Date

This story is a gentle reminder that we all were young and less wise and discerning a decade or two ago. Let's focus on the positive attributes that can come out of the giftings in our teenagers and try to treat them like a potential world changer already. Your goal on this date is to see how they view themselves and look for any opportunity to speak in faith what you see they can become and already are with their unique personality!

Personal Reflections

Date Questions

Offense Check: Is there anything in your heart that I do, have done, or have not done in the past that irritated, belittled, hurt, shamed, angered, or let you down that might hinder you from trusting me and opening up on our date today?

1. Do you consider yourself an extrovert who likes to be with people to relax and unwind or more of an introvert who prefers to be alone when you relax and recharge?

2. Do you prefer to be in charge of a project, or would you rather assist in a group?

3. What lack of character in others bugs you the most?

4. What frustrates you most in a group project?

5. Do you consider yourself more of a visionary, server, leader, encourager, or teacher?

6. Do you tend to think more about what's happening right now or about what could happen in the future?

7. Do you get more accomplished when you are all alone or when others are around?

8. What would your idea of a great evening be?

9. How has your birth order in the family affected you positively and negatively?

10. What personality type do you tend to think would be helpful or fun to have in a spouse to encourage or balance you out?

☕ Who would you enjoy seeing in a live performance?

Closing Question

And now I'd like to give you the opportunity to ask me any questions you have.

Spoken Blessing

I bless you for what your personality brings to our home and family and for who you are naturally when people let you feel safe to be yourself. I want to be one of those who welcomes the real you and appreciates and celebrates how you were designed by our Maker. I want to walk with you as we become aware of the weaknesses that are your personality's tendencies, giving grace and encouragement to overcome. I want you to feel free to be yourself with us.

Responses to Remember

Date 6:

Discovering Their Spiritual Gifts

If this young adult has never made a confession of faith as a Christian, you may want to skip over this date. According to Ephesians 4:8 and Acts 2:38–39, spiritual gifts are given in the Holy Spirit Package when one confesses with your mouth that "Jesus is Lord and believe in your heart that God hath raised Him from the dead, they then will be saved" (paraphrased from Romans 10:9).

Parent Tip

Do you ever feel like your teenage children abide mostly in their bedroom and bathroom, and if they saunter through the kitchen into the garage, you ponder what you might say or do in that brief moment to connect with them or show them you love and miss them? I have been working on resisting the urge to pounce on my young adults when they finally come into my sphere, like a spider sensing action in her web, lest they try to avoid the areas of the house where I'm hanging out in the future.

If you are a parent or grandparent to some of this socially active generation of youth, then you understand my desire to have as many two-way conversations as you can when you are finally physically in the same space. Group-messaging apps are very helpful in communication, but face-to-face is still the clearest and best form without questions of intent.

I recall a time when, passing through the kitchen and finding my son cooking again, I decided to "pounce gingerly" for the second time in a week and ask if he had any feedback for me on how us parents have either overlooked or helped affirm spiritual gifts in our children.

While stirring his sizzling mixture, he thought and then kindly gave me this condensed report between his lunch bites perched at the bar.

He shared how certain spiritual gifts are more easily recognized, practiced, and praised than others because of the results being tangibly seen. Parents can easily recognize, call out, and rely on certain spiritual gifts because of how they make life go smoother for everyone and create a better experience emotionally, physically, or visually. Some of these often praised ones are serving, organization, or administration, giving, leadership, mercy, pastor, or loyal relational listeners, exhortation or encouragement, teaching, or words of knowledge. The more subtle ones that we need as well but that can seem to make our life more difficult or confusing are those who naturally discern wrong motives and thinking. Prophetic and warning or seemingly always cautious, controversial, futuristic, or serious, apostolic or having a bigger picture, supernatural manifestations in words, prayers, healings, or other signs of the Holy Spirit working. Evangelists can make us uncomfortable when constantly bringing eternity up to strangers or speaking of the story of the cross and Christ's suffering more than some prefer.

Some of the ways our family has overlooked and not always recognized or given heed to a gift of discernment is when we are discussing scenarios. If one of the children suggested another view of what may have been unfolding or happening in one or more of the involved people's hearts and minds that differs from our way of thinking or set of values, we may have brushed it off never thinking twice that what was said only once, in humility, is actually a huge key needed for the expedient outlook or outcome. Often a person with this gift may seem to defend the other party from judgment or make us feel uncomfortable with the suggestions or opposite thinking they offer.

Another way our family may have misread our prophets and teachers is when they tend to "find the bones in the meat of a message" or sense a red flag for something that we all were excited about and planning to go ahead with. It may feel like they always find something negative or have a burden, but it is for the purpose of intercession and warning.

A teacher may view missing content and lack of explanation or clarity in a teaching as compromising and misleading people. A true fact or detail omitted by a speaker seems obvious and big to them, while we may never even have thought of it or deemed it important.

Sometimes as parents we gave more weight to the older, louder voices and missed some of our quiet, wise, younger ones. These younger voices have often learned a lot over time from needing to just listen and have much valuable feedback we may be robbing ourselves of by not waiting patiently to hear more fully from each one.

Personal Reflections

Before the Date

After you discuss and discern what some of their spiritual gifts are, take time to pray that this child will walk in their gifts in the Spirit of honor and humility. In total abandonment of any credit, response, outcome, or fruits.

Date Questions

Offense Check: Is there anything in your heart that I do, have done, or have not done in the past that irritated, belittled, hurt, shamed, angered, or let you down that might hinder you from trusting me and opening up on our date today?

1. What would you say are a few of your spiritual gifts?

2. What would be your main goal or motivation of results for the recipients when you use your gifts?

   For example: Is it to comfort or encourage? Do you want them to know the truth? Get free from bondages? Be eternally safe? Be healed? Repent or know someone cares? This would help you know what your dominant motivational gift is while you use and function in other spiritual gifts.

3. Would you rather teach a class, serve refreshments, surprise someone with a gift, write encouraging words in a card, offer a back rub, or organize a small group to meet weekly?

4. If you were to visit a sick person in the hospital, how would you try to encourage them?

   - By offering advice on what to do to get better
   - By offering to take care of their pets or things at the house while they are gone
   - By encouraging them that God is with them in this
   - By preparing a nice gift and card or money for them
   - By rubbing their stiff muscles
   - By listening to them share the story of their accident

5. What do you usually see as a need in your church that is not happening enough?

6. What burdens do you have for our community, and how would you want to get involved and make a difference?

7. Have you sensed that the Holy Spirit might be prompting you to approach someone but weren't sure if it was His voice or if you had the courage to follow through?

8. What ideas come to your mind for solutions to circumstances or people's needs?

9. What is your favorite book and character in the Bible?

10. Have you experienced supernatural things in your life that are beyond you and really seemed like God was involved?

 Who in history would you love to meet and ask some questions?

Closing Question

And now I'd like to give you the opportunity to ask me any questions you have.

Spoken Blessing

Father, I call to life the gifts of the Spirit that you put into (child's name) _____________ for the edifying of God's people and bringing more souls into faith in Jesus Christ. I pray (he or she) will walk in your authority but always in humility, honoring your name and others above (his or herself) in the powerful name of Jesus.

Schedule

Take time to look at your next month's schedule, discuss with your child the next possible date, and pencil it in the index calendar as well as your planner or phone calendar.

Responses to Remember

Date 7:

Love Language™

Parent Tip

It was after another great service at our home church, and I was enjoying a quick catch-up chat with my friend whom I hadn't seen for a few weeks. Her twenty-three-year-old son came up behind her, slinging one arm around her shoulder, wearing his big grin. We paused our conversation to give him our attention. Unlike the usual, "Mom, let's go, I am hungry," from waiting children, his question was, "What vegetables do we have to go with the meat I am making for our lunch?"

This hunter, chef, and carpenter is the same fellow that smiled on a weekend night when his mom finally finished her work and settled on the living room couch, where he could lean on her while she tousled his head full of raven hair. This youngest child was one of the last two still living at home out of the five children. He seemed to be natural at mediating and reconciling any differences that came up between family members or friends.

He was a childhood friend to my sons who played airsoft in the woods, shared birthday parties and gifts, and spent time in the creek together. Once they were older and owned motorcycles, they would ride the Blue Ridge Parkway on Sunday afternoons or go for a short summer ride up the mountain for ice cream. He would invite them over for a winter hot tub night, watching movies and snacking out under the stars. The family is very musical, with someone strumming and him being no exception in that he loved to sing along and groove to any song familiar to him. Any debate or argument with this friend was always with smiles and laughter before, during, and after. Sunday afternoon the group of young men enjoyed rounds of disc golf at the same park where they had played as toddlers. The next two nights found him at the gym playing Spikeball while offering around the beef jerky he had made earlier.

Before leaving for a youth event one evening, this son carried his empty bowl of chicken noodle soup to the sink and thanked his mom for the delicious supper. Why am I highlighting his personality and strengths, and what does this have to do with Love Languages™? His character, Love Languages™, gifts, and deeds have been talked about more than ever before in the last three days because we cannot experience them here ever again. He was ushered into eternity forty-eight hours ago as I write this condensed version of his fine young life. Many of us are grieving the gravity of losing him in our lives during this thing called time in our Gregorian calendar.

Before the Date

As my husband and I walk through this new experience with our young adult children and their great loss, there is a flood of memories, gratitude, and appreciation when they arrive home at the end of the day. We discuss our friend who has passed, and the moments we had together, and laugh and cry and think of all he was and did in his twenty-three years. How he always kept the campfires going from dawn to dusk and suggested the most exotic meats for the camping committee menu. We mourn the dreams he never realized before he left earth, like opening his own food truck.

As we celebrate his life and mourn his loss, it causes me to look at our own children and ask: how can we appreciate them while they are here with us? How can we speak their Love Language™? Time with your children is precious. Be present with them. Show them the deep affection you feel for them. Even if it feels awkward, learn to speak their Love Language™. Having your child with you is a privilege.

Personal Reflections

Date Questions

Offense Check: Is there anything in your heart that I do, have done, or have not done in the past that irritated, belittled, hurt, shamed, angered, or let you down that might hinder you from trusting me and opening up on our date today?

1. If someone wanted to show you they are interested in getting to know you better, what would be your favorite way for them to do that?

2. If someone wanted to show you they care about you, how could they communicate that best to you?

3. How do you best cultivate the friendships you do have currently?

4. What are the two kindest or most thoughtful things someone has done for you?

5. Who are the two people in your life you feel the most love from and why?

6. What communication, action, or lack of communication or action has tended to hurt you the most easily in the past?

7. How do you tend to hear from God? Through Scripture verses, songs, pictures He gives you, nature, gifts, protection, provision, stories, or analogies any other way?

8. What are three things people do that make you feel disrespected or uncared for?

9. Would you rather I surprise you with a thoughtful personal gift, a back, foot, or scalp rub, a note with encouragement about who you are, helping with a project you are doing, or fun time spent away with me?

10. What is something you have seen or heard parents do for their children that would sound exciting to you?

🥤 Would you rather be in an eating contest of corn on the cob, steak, gummy bears, cotton candy, salted chocolate caramels, York mints, PB&J Uncrustables, or shrimp?

From these thoughts, I suspect your two main Love Languages™ (from ***The 5 Love Languages: The Secret to Love that Lasts*** by Dr. Gary Chapman) are:

-Acts of Service™
-Quality Time™
-Words of Affirmation™
-Physical Touch™
-Gifts™

Closing Question

And now I'd like to give you the opportunity to ask me any questions you have.

Child's Closing Prayer

Lord, thank you that someone cares about what my Love Language™ is and wants to keep learning how to love me well. Help my (mom, dad, grandparent, or mentor) _______________ to understand and remember in what ways I feel loved the most but not to feel pressured or condemned when they forget at times. Help me to think about how I can best show love to those closest to me as well. Thank you that you know these details about all of us and don't want us hurting each other, but to feel cared for and to love each other well. In Jesus's name, Amen.

Schedule

Take time to look at your next month's schedule, discuss with your child the next possible date, and pencil it in the index calendar as well as your planner or phone calendar.

Responses to Remember

Date 8:

Life Message

My Story

I tried to be calm and act normal as my dad sat down across from me at the small round table, opening the hinged lid of his black Aladdin lunch box. As a grown woman in my thirties, it didn't seem like it should be so hard to call my dad and ask to meet for lunch. As unusual and awkward as it seemed in our relationship, he had agreed to meet and asked me to come to the lunchroom where he was working as a groundskeeper at a hotel and fitness center.

The meeting arose out of a desire I had for a closer relationship with my father. I had come to grips with how much a child's relationship and view of themself and God the Father is related to one's experience in relationship with our earthly father. This journey toward winning and seeking my dad's heart began more intentionally at nineteen, after my confession of Jesus as Savior. That year going into my twentieth year was the hardest year of my fifty years so far. I did not realize God was forging my "life message" through the fire of it. My new desire to now honor my parents because of Jesus, yet not necessarily join their denomination, formed a heat for one of the first and hardest tests I've passed through. I wanted to be willing to do hard and sacrificial things that the Holy Spirit was leading me to for honor's sake, in spite of not really having peers around me that felt called to do the same things.

Your Influence

When we are obedient and victorious in an area, it gives us authority to teach and require it of others whom we disciple later. It certainly contributed to my life message today that includes calling people to honor everyone in our lives, including our authorities, no matter how difficult or even ungodly they appear. The purpose for this book came after I more fully recognized how the void of not feeling known and understood affected my life as an adult.

I desire to encourage parents in caring for and listening intentionally to their children in all areas of their life and throughout the different seasons and stages of the child's life. This is still my desire to relate heart-to-heart and honestly with my eighty-three-year-old parents. My husband and I still have ongoing sweet opportunities to cultivate this culture and lifestyle with our five adult children, their spouses and children, and others whom we get to influence or mentor.

His Story

My husband experienced a radical conversion to Jesus Christ during our dating years as well. He walked out of a lifestyle that included rebellion, alcohol, smoking, drugs, ungodly thinking and words, and a mind filled with heavy metal rock music, immorality, and violent action movies. Now he ministers with understanding to unconverted people with addictions, street lifestyles, and similar mentalities.

As his closest friend, I observe that my husband's strengths of influence today include the opposite of the arrogance, pride, and independence he used to live by as I now see him walking in dependence to the Holy Spirit, humility, reverence, and honor to others. Dave's life message reverberates to do all we do out of our love for our God and Savior and that it all be carried out in excellence, in a spirit of honor and humility, and always toward reconciliation of relationships. This is to be applied no matter who your adversaries or conflict is with or even why.

Your Life Message

In retrospect, I see this formed during his younger years when the zeal barometer was high. He walked through the effective character-building process of "death of a vision." I saw the importance of a life partner's role in that season, to believe in and affirm the vision God gave the partner while helping them to see a bigger hand directing through disagreeable coworkers or authorities, and being open to constructive criticism to help improve character and quality of output.

This concept is true whether we are single adults walking through this hard time with a friend or mentee or parents walking with our own children. Honesty in love is better than flattery. Encouraging someone to wallow in self-pity by affirming an unhealthy victim mentality will only set them back in life. As we all face some misunderstandings, differences, or insensitive actions or words—which we have all been guilty of ourselves—there is perspective and response that builds our life message into a very effective one when we can see it as God allowing us to be tested and reproved to a higher standard, no matter how terrible the delivery is or by whom.

When we choose not to retaliate or run but to look into with discernment for the truths in the accusation, criticism, or rejection, we can pray for grace to receive it and work on the lack or receive healing for the lie that is causing our negative coping response. Any character you have allowed God to develop in you can help you more tenderly respond to other people's hardships while also giving you authority to demonstrate and teach faithfulness on this subject.

Your Child's Life Message

We see how God often weaves these same strengths of character and values into the lives of the next generation to exemplify it in their life messages, communicated to their generation with terms and illustrations relatable to them.

Our oldest daughter wrote a book encouraging women and girls what they can do on their part to cultivate their father-daughter relationship. This came out of her own challenging experience in our home during those transitional years when your relationship changes from being daddy's cute little girl to swoop up in his arms to becoming a young adult needing a shoulder-to-shoulder relationship to openly discuss new subjects. The tests we pass rather than bypass form an applicable life message.

Personal Reflections

Before the Date

Most degrees acquired, businesses opened, ministries sprouted, and strong convictions formed come out of something that was a big struggle at one point. You experienced and prevailed through the dark tunnel into the light. So as you think about yourself and your child on the date with you, what hardship have you experienced that gave you fresh burdens, resolve, or goals you didn't have before? What is the message He has formed through testing you or your child? How will many others benefit from your obedience?

Date Questions

Offense Check: Is there anything in your heart that I do, have done, or have not done in the past that irritated, belittled, hurt, shamed, angered, or let you down that might hinder you from trusting me and opening up on our date today?

1. What are a few things that burden you the most in our world today?

2. What would be some ideas or ways you would love to get involved to solve some of those problems?

3. If money was no obstacle, what ministry or business platform for influence would you love to see happen in your future?

4. Which group would you be most drawn to help and encourage?
    - fatherless children
    - poor or homeless people
    - unbelievers
    - inmates
    - inner-city kids
    - gangs
    - abused children
    - orphans
    - prostitutes
    - handicapped people
    - elderly people
    - sick people
    - young children

5. Would you rather speak to or teach a group, sing praises, coach a team, share your life story to help others, give presents, physically help out, or pray with hurting people?

6. What attributes would you hope for in a life partner for your life calling if God has marriage in mind for you?

7. If you could give the president, senators, governors, or mayors some advice on how to lead our country and communities, what would you say?

8. What are some little mundane things you are trying to be intentional about and faithful in, hoping God will entrust you with bigger things soon?

9. What's the biggest compliment you ever got or could get?

10. Even if it seems frivolous, can you put into words how you dream or envision your future life partner and marriage if you could choose?

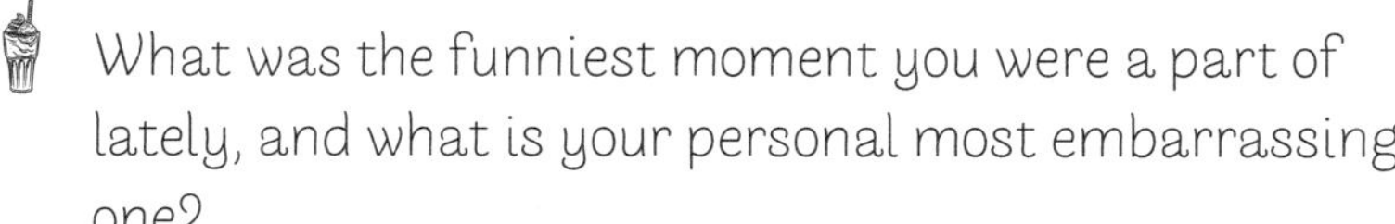 What was the funniest moment you were a part of lately, and what is your personal most embarrassing one?

Closing Question

And now I'd like to give you the opportunity to ask me any questions you have.

Spoken Blessing

I believe God has put in you natural abilities as well as skills you've learned along the way. Most of all, I believe God has brought you through some hurdles that will help you relate to certain people and circumstances to make a difference.

Pray or speak a blessing on the child for their future and some attributes you see in their life that will help them influence the world for good.

Schedule

Take time to look at your next month's schedule, discuss with your child the next possible date, and pencil it in the index calendar as well as your planner or phone calendar.

Responses to Remember

Recognizing Lies

My Story

I stood in our dining room discussing some document I had emailed for Dave to print out at the office. I felt very triggered and wanted to respond to his comments about the format of the content in anger. I walked into the living room to get perspective before I hurt my soul mate as much or more than I felt he was hurting me.

I perched on the front of the suede armchair's cushion by the fireplace, asking God why we seem to always have conflict around documents I compose with my self-taught computer skills. Did I not have a teachable spirit? Was I not humble enough to receive constructive criticism? Why do I so frequently feel dumb? Why did something rise up in me that wanted to lash out when I felt foolish? At that moment, I thought the way he addressed what I needed to do differently felt so uncaring and unkind. I was under the impression that his strong, administrative personality was demeaning me, without that being his actual heart or goal.

My husband works with ten other employees daily in an office as director of Gospel Express Ministries whenever we are not touring or doing itinerant ministry. I did have to take into consideration that the root may be within me since there seemed to be very little conflict with his office staff. I asked God why it's so painful for me and why I am so sensitive to corrections on my projects. We ended up needing to put a bandage on our episode of contention while he went to work and I was carrying out my duties at home.

Later, after supper dishes and little children's baths were done, we once again met to process as we had planned. After going back into the vicious cycle as both of us tried to share our feelings, desires, and goals, we dispersed in desperation into separate bedrooms to cry out to God for answers. Neither of us enjoyed the lack of understanding or conclusion we were getting out or putting in.

The Revelation

After pouring my feelings and heart out to God, my husband finally joined me on the floor at the foot of our bed. He asked God to give him compassion for me and through that loving prayer and some time ministering to me, God gave me a picture of a memory that released our answer! I saw a little girl and her two sisters on top of a large wooden workbench. It was my father's tin shop where he manufactured some of his own customized ductwork for his heating and air-conditioning business. The daughters were asked to each take hold of a side of the large tin square, carefully avoiding the sharp edges that could slice through soft fingers.

As my father was using the drill to screw a corner together, my side probably moved because I was avoiding too much pressure on the sharp end with my hand. I remember my dad's frustrated face as he looked up and said, disgusted, "Not like that!" in Pennsylvania Dutch. I felt fear and shame that I could not please my father and had let him down.

In that room with my husband, I wept like I was that little girl again. Those shameful feelings saying, "you're so dumb" and "why don't you know better?" had originated from this childhood experience. My Heavenly Father cared enough to reveal how He is reversing that lie about myself for me. Once the revelation came and the tears were done, I felt totally healed. It felt like that unworthy, dumb identity was no longer on me.

Now I can respond to corrections with no fear of rejection, aware that I have nothing to lose when I don't do something well or perfectly right. I am much more comfortable being wrong, not being talented or knowledgeable in areas, because I feel more loved and settled in who I am according to my Maker, Savior, and Comforter. I am amazed how free I feel now when someone else does something better than me.

Before the Date

The story is not to blame anyone or put fear in any parents but rather to testify that when God brings revelation of a core fear or lie that was received years ago, you will experience a closure and debunking of that lie.

Make sure you take time to ask God personally about why you tend to experience the same few negative feelings from people. He might bring resolution to it. There is an index resource in the back of the book called "Heart Care" that has steps on how to allow God to be your therapist by asking Him if there is a memory He can reveal to you. This memory can be the origin of your belief in a lie that is associated with the painful or negative emotion you keep feeling when you are not treated perfectly. We become better people to live with and relate to when our past does not affect our responses to our loved ones' character or lack thereof at times.

Date Questions

Offense Check: Is there anything in your heart that I do, have done, or have not done in the past that irritated, belittled, hurt, shamed, angered, or let you down that might hinder you from trusting me and opening up on our date today?

1. Has anyone offended you in a way that you really feel like justice should be served?

2. Do you remember a time that one of us parents hurt your feelings or shut you down?

3. What is something that will shut you down quickly?

4. What situations do you try to avoid because it feels awkward or scary? Why?

5. Is there someone in particular that you prefer to avoid? Why?

6. What would you say is the most traumatic thing you've experienced? How has that affected your thinking?

7. Do you consider yourself creative, talented, and wise? If not, why not?

8. Do you like the way God created you? What part is hard to embrace at times?

9. Are there certain circumstances that seem to bring more feelings of rejection than normal?

10. Who do you feel the most relaxed, safe, and able to be yourself with? Why?

 If you were stuck for a week in a tent on a cliff with no electronic devices and could choose only one thing in each category, what would you choose?

Categories: A person, a food item, a drink, a book.

Closing Question

And now I'd like to give you the opportunity
     to ask me any questions you have.

Spoken Blessing

God, I thank you for this young adult you have brought into my life. Thank you for what I have learned about life because _______ is in my life. I am thankful you know the best way to love (him or her) and have a specific way that you speak and care for (him or her) because of it. Help me to study (him or her) and be more aware what means a lot to (their name) _______. I pray (he or she) will have grace when we as adults keep forgetting and at times miss the mark. Thank you for how you made ___________ (their name) and for our time together, may (he or she) know (he or she) is loved and special to me and you.

Responses to Remember

Sacred Things

I remember driving away from a great week at a family conference when one of our daughters knelt between the two front seats of the motor home to share about her week with her father and me. Among the testimonies, teachings, and challenges received, she had felt inspired to make a vow of singleness to the Lord until she was twenty years old. My husband and I were quite surprised at the thought since she had not consulted us before making the vow, and we would have probably only recommended waiting to court until eighteen. She carried the faith that if the right man for her future called earlier, he could surely wait until then if it was meant to be.

Although she herself would not currently recommend going so far as to vow, I do believe God honored her faith as a preteen to serve Him and trust Him with her future. The results were that she could focus unhindered on skills to cultivate and subjects to study further for her serving opportunities and ministry for the next eight years. Not saying she never had boy crushes or mental drama about them, but no guy ever tried to ask her out or called her father until the week she turned twenty. That was amazing to me.

We have had various experiences with our children

waiting on that right life partner, and we don't claim to have the answers. Currently we still have three honorable, devoted, handsome men in their twenties landing at our house between all their work, ministry, and social travels. Our youngest daughter of eighteen, along with us parents, love the experience of all doing life together as adults with individual callings and giftings until any more of them move away. I give this background to share some viewpoints we offered concerning the facts of life and reproduction for the next generation.

Biblical Worldview

The prison ministry our family has served under for twenty-three years helped create a biblical worldview for our children as they got to interact with many inmates all through childhood. They each heard and saw firsthand the ongoing pain of rejection, harm, and consequences of fatherlessness. Their friends were from a variety of families, from one child to twenty children in the home, with some educated as homeschoolers, others in private schools, and yet others in public schools. Their cultures included Amish, Mennonite, Full Gospel, and nondenominational.

Our son has lead worship in the Love Life prayer and awareness services beside the biggest abortion clinic in the south in Charlotte, NC. We all go as a family and hear and see firsthand the sacredness of life and the immorality and lack of responsibility from men and women that causes people to overlook it. We cry and pray as the clinic opens and cars pull in to meet their appointment for the snuffing of the life inside. I recommend all families to participate in the clinic closest to you, it made the need to overturn *Roe v. Wade* in all the states real to our children. In *Darwin and Lady Hope: The Untold Story*, author L. R. Croft writes that Darwin supposedly recanted of his evolution theory on his deathbed. In the same way, Jane Roe has tried to reverse, with tears, what her trial legalized in the United States. I recommend watching a film called *Unwanted*, which helps innocent, protected children visualize what the mother goes through to have an abortion and why the mother would feel the need to have one.

Our family took in a week of seminars and all the expos at Ken Ham's Creation Museum and Ark as well as watched many educational movies on Creation, which builds on the Genesis view of marriage and intimacy. These ways of exposing our children to both what we believe and those who challenge them can help the next generation form moral convictions. Above all, your story and your siblings and parents' stories of moral freedom or failure and its consequences, good or bad, will probably influence your children more than any other testimony in history. As you go on this date, keep in mind who and how you were at their age and keep a kind and approachable face if your teenager does open up and become vulnerable and honest.

Before the Date

Look back and remember how your parents warned you of sexual sin or how you wish your parents would have discussed this subject with you. Knowing the great parent you want to be, speak with confidence, honor, and integrity as the one who loves them enough to push past the uncomfortable.

I believe they need to hear from you how sweet, beautiful, worshipful, guilt-free, and bonding intimacy is when kept sacred and experienced only in the covenant marriage.

Date Questions

Offense Check: Is there anything in your heart that I do, have done, or have not done in the past that irritated, belittled, hurt, shamed, angered, or let you down that might hinder you from trusting me and opening up on our date today?

1. Fatherlessness has become the root problem and main hurt and hindrance to many individuals in our American Society. What do you see as something that could prevent this?

2. What is one thing about your birth setting that you are grateful for and one thing that has been hard to accept at times?

3. If you could have chosen what era of the world you could be born in, which would sound exciting or easier to you?

4. Do you feel accepted and feel like people enjoy who you are? And by whom? If not, why not?

5. What characteristics or features do you see in yourself from either one of your parents?

6. Have you found grace to keep yourself pure for your future marriage partner? What is your main area of struggle in purity?

7. In what ways are you tempted, and how could I/we encourage and support you to live in moral victory?

8. Has anyone ever introduced you to porn or masturbation?

9. Would you be open to having accountability conversations periodically with one of us parents or mentors?

10. When you picture yourself as a parent, what thoughts go through your mind? What are some of your goals if you become a parent?

 If you could dream where to go on your honeymoon and some goals while on it, what might that look like?

Closing Question

And now I'd like to give you the opportunity to ask me any questions you have.

Spoken Blessing

I am so glad God brought you into my life and that we can share about these things on an adult level. I pray you will keep knowing more and more who God made you to be and experience how He wants to give you the grace to pass all the tests you will face and wants you to be fulfilled as you choose the high road. I pray He will illuminate the paths you should take when you come to deciding cross-roads and that His peace will guide you. I pray you will learn to use caution when He gives you red flags and wait on Him to give you green lights. I pray you can embrace his chosen gender for you and celebrate it by keep-ing yourself pure for that special life partner someday. Please feel free to come to me about any struggles, tests, or questions you may face in the future.

Schedule

Congratulations! If you took the dates in order, you have now completed all the subjects we offer for this age level! If you have not completed all the earlier dates for this age level, you can continue having them in the order and pace you prefer.

Responses to Remember

COLLEGE & CAREER
AGES 19 & UP

POSITION OF ADULT ROLE:

Supporter, communication initiator, friend, and cheer-leader. You are further releasing this young adult to make decisions, wise and unwise, fun and disappointing, scary or encouraging.

This is a testing time for you to be more aware than ever to not look to this child for your fulfillment, dreams, needs, or well-being but to think unselfishly about what is best for them. This is a good time to look into your own life for any unhealthy thinking or parenting you might need to face, change, and apologize for.

You will want to discern what it takes to break down any walls they may have put up in the past months or years and work on maintaining or establishing a safe relationship between you two in these fleeting years before they marry or move away. To treat them respectfully with trust, as you would other adults, can help empower your young adult child to rise to the challenge of living responsibly and earning their age-appropriate independence.

Creating a Safe Place

My expressionless teenage daughter passed me in the hall with a deep-throated groan. In an hour, her obligations as vocalist and musician for the worship team would pull her on stage in a crowded tent. She had finally been able to be with her western friends in person and didn't want to leave that opportunity. I felt like I may have failed to remind this young girl she needed some white mind space and bodily rest before her evening responsibilities. I mentioned that I should have texted her to come back and take a nap, which only brought more frustration. I tried to reassure her that I was not blaming her, but it was too late, and my rationalizing wasn't helping.

Have you ever been perplexed trying to fix and comfort your anxious child, but it seemed like you only heightened their stress level? What could I have done to be a safer place for her in this hard circumstance?

It took her older brother kindly pulling me aside to explain how I hindered more than helped, even if my motive was good. Here was his perceptive viewpoint. When I brought up how I should have reminded her to come back and rest, she heard, "If you would have been wise and acted like a responsible adult, you would have come back and rested so you are not as tired as you are now. It was your fault."

Was that what I was meaning to say? No, I was trying to take the blame on myself and comfort her! Before we go into how I could have been a safer place for her, let's look at how we both have filters formed by our life experiences.

One of my filters, or lies, I had experienced from my youth was that it was my fault when others around me weren't happy or even acting wise or kind. This resulted in me going through life with a victim mentality. Do you notice how when my daughter wasn't feeling happy and well-taken care of, I processed that it was probably a fault in my mothering? I parented through my filter of "it's surely my fault," and so I need to apologize for her discomfort and hardship.

If I was my best, healthy self, I would have recognized that she is old enough and has shown enough maturity in the past to make wise choices. She doesn't need me to hover over her. I can be Jesus to her by showing compassion and sympathy, then speaking encouraging words like "you got this, girl" but not mentioning what could have been different since she is well aware of how to prevent this scenario.

My son went on to remind me that if all he and his siblings do on these ministry trips is say no to fun social things in order to perform and minister at an excellent level, they will burn out. In other words, if all we do is sleep and minister, we will be in a deeper depression than her temporary feeling of tiredness from too much time with friends. Ouch. Us grown-ups would all be healthier if we apply that to our lives!

In this scenario, we also take into consideration that my daughter may have a filter with how she heard or received my response when she was tired. She may have had past experiences of feeling misunderstood, judged, or accused and took my response to mean she had let me down, wasn't responsible or wise enough, or wasn't working hard enough. Do you see how we all hear through filters of interpretation according to our past repetitive negative emotions in circumstances?

I am not insinuating that every negative emotion you feel in circumstances links back to a lie you have believed about yourself, life, others, or God. What I am saying is that if you repeatedly want to react and can't respond well to feeling the same three or four negative emotions, you may want to give those some extra attention to where they might stem from by using "Heart Care" in the index and look inward instead of outward. With these tools, you can help yourself and then others problem solve relational conflict and cause your loved ones to feel more understood.

Before the Date

Whether it's repeated conflict or stress between you and your child or your spouse, you are wise and will be a healthier you when you take time for inventory of your own emotional well-being. Go to the "Heart Care" page in the index and remember your latest big episode between your child and you. Take note of and process the negative emotion you felt to see what your filter may be.

Perceiving this child's words and actions through a filter at times can amplify discord between you. See the Index under "Care Cycle" and "End of Day" journaling for healthy steps to take care of each one's own repeated negative emotions and where they might be coming from.

My husband and I attempted to create a culture in our

family where we do not dismiss strong attitudes and ig-nore negative feelings or reactions any more than we no-tice and acknowledge happiness and celebrations.

Because our ministry is often in public and life happens, we choose to address inner conflict when and where it happens before we speak or minister to others. My hus-band believes, and has taught and modeled well in our family, we should avoid unresolved conflict or sin in our life because it may well hinder the anointing of God in our life.

Although we addressed conflict, we at times ended up misunderstanding and hurting each other more through the redemption process because of one mistake in how we processed. The steps we took as we cared for each oth-er's hearts included what felt like blame or accusation that called for defending instead of caring. Like so many rela-tionships that try to process instead of stuffing feelings, we would often end up in the vicious cycle. We realize now each one of us often were no longer feeling safe in some of these conversations. We thank God for the tool that Focus on the Family gleaned from their many years of experi-ence and use in their "Marriage Intensive" program.

The key is what not to do!

Do not repeat or quote specific, detailed actions or words that the offended observes that the "offender" did to avoid the offender from needing to correct or defend what actually was done or meant. Whenever someone feels wrongly accused, the conversation turns from caring for the heart to feeling like a courtroom with a defendant and prosecutor, and that does not usually end in a win-win situation.

1. **The Offended is the First Speaker**. Instead of the hurt one replaying what was said or done by the offender, they only say one or two words to describe the negative emotion they felt .

2. **The Offender is the First Listener.** Maintaining eye contact and listening carefully without interrupting validates and acknowledges that the negative feeling was real to the offended. Regardless of the offender's pure motives, they validate how the offended felt and express they are sorry their child experienced that from the exchange.

3. **The other mentality that was very freeing for us is that most of us have filters.** We filter how we hear things through a flawed identity stemming from past offenses from others that God wants to heal. The responsibility is on the listener to take care of his own feelings when people are around them and circumstances and words are not perfectly or honorably stated. We all have filters that have formed from lies we believed about who we are after we were mistreated or spoken to a certain way. These lies and unhealthy views of ourselves and others creates conflict between human beings more than just disagreements.

We learned the concept that we all are responsible for cleaning up our "own yards" but can keep "the gate" open for those whom we trust and feel safe with to "let them in" and help us find healing. It was revolutionary to me when I was told I don't need to take the blame for all the things my husband feels if I don't communicate perfectly. I always had the mentality growing up that when working things out, we needed to figure out who was at fault. Blame and accusation started in the Garden after the Fall, and it is never from the Holy Kingdom. Honesty, responsibility, humility, honor, and confession all are and were exemplified by Jesus, except for the fact that he never had to confess being or acting wrong .

Since we all are trying to take responsibility for what we feel when someone speaks while still communicating in honor, it has simplified our discussions and personal run-ins at our house. Taking responsibility for how you feel and not projecting it onto others really minimizes conflict and confusion. Today you have the opportunity to listen to your young adult and see how you can possibly be a safer person to them. To learn more about this concept go to www.focusonthefamily.com/hoperestored.

Personal Reflections

Date Questions

Offense Check: Is there anything in your heart that I do, have done, or have not done in the past that irritated, belittled, hurt, shamed, angered, or let you down that might hinder you from trusting me and opening up on our date today?

1. What would you say was your most exciting or fun event in the last month?

2. What is the biggest concern, stress, or trial right now?

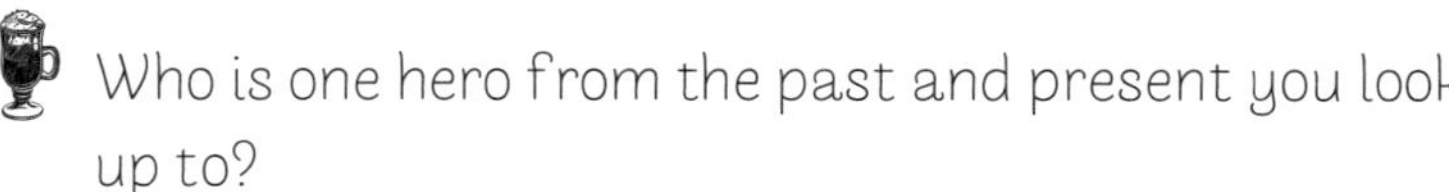 Who is one hero from the past and present you look up to?

3. Who do you tend to go to during a hard time, and what is it about them that makes you feel comfortable with them?

4. Are there things I do or have done that tend to put up a wall between us?

5. What are some ways you don't feel like I am hearing and understanding you?

6. Is there something we as parents have promised that we never carried out?

What is the funniest thing you watched or heard lately?

7. Has there ever been a time that you did not feel protected by us as parents?

8. Is there anything significant that happened while you were young that is still affecting your self-identity or perception of others today?

 What characteristics in a person would help you trust them and want to get to know them more to maybe consider courting?

9. What is one thing I could do monthly to be an encouragement to you?

10. Do you have any suggestions for what we can both bring to build a safer and more supportive role in each other's relationship?

 What is your favorite table game currently, and what about it do you enjoy?

Closing Question

Now I am also open if there're any questions you've been wanting to ask me.

Spoken Blessing

Thank you for spending this time with me and for what you shared. I treasured having this time with just the two of us.

I want you to feel emotionally, spiritually, and mentally safe. Your feelings, ideas, and concerns matter to us. I want you to be able to be vulnerable without fear of me ever using the information against you. I want us to have a culture between us where both our personalities, perspectives, and goals are welcomed and valued even when they differ. I want you to be able to share thoughts and ideas without fear of ridicule or rejection.

Do you sense any manipulation or fear on my part in releasing you as an adult?

Responses to Remember

Who You "Be"

I shifted my weight from the kneeling position to sitting on the carpeted floor in front of our bedroom window, where I try to align and exchange my heart and motives with Heaven's before I start my days. I was attempting to think of the different names of God as I reverently came before His throne. Scanning my memory for name meanings that correlated with what all He had been to me lately, my mind jumped to the line in the song, "He Knows My Name." I wondered who the Lord knows me as if He would call me by name. I knew friends across the ocean who had changed their tribal names to Bible names after converting to Christianity. I knew that my family, relatives, church families, and neighbors all called me by my first name only during my childhood. I had grown up hearing my older relatives pronounce the ending consonant with the distinct influence of their German dialect.

After I jumped out of the school world into the work scene, my new manager tagged my second name onto my first to distinguish me from the other Ruth at work. I also started dating and attending a different church in that teenage era and was introduced to people by my boyfriend and coworkers as Ruth Ann. So through the next decades, I found myself considering which season of my life people got to know me to help me determine which way would be most appropriate to sign their Christmas cards, Ruth or Ruth Ann.

As I came before the Lord that morning, I stopped and seriously asked Jesus how *He* says my name. I was quiet. What popped into my head next was a total surprise. It was neither the German "Ruz" or Ruth or Ruth Ann but a totally different name!

I bounded downstairs to get online and look up what the name meant. The meaning put me in awe and left me feeling so understood I wept. The definition I read that day described wholly who I am when I am free to be myself, without fear of critics hemming me in.

I have treasured how God looks at me and what He calls me so much that it is the only secret I have ever kept from my closest friend, my husband, Dave. I have never shared it with anyone and will treasure it always till I see my Savior face-to-face. I so look forward to not having to imagine Him when I worship and talk to Him. I choose to believe, in faith, that He was truly speaking to me that day. If I heard wrong about what He calls me, then we can throw our heads back and have a good laugh together when we're face-to-face!

I often laugh with Him from down here when I sense it was a good one for Him to watch unfold from His foreknowledge and upper view of what I just experienced. Sometimes it's the way He answers my prayer by blowing it out of the water. Other times, I picture Him witnessing what I like to call one of my hilarious, spontaneous "bloopers" throughout my life. I just can't quite see the twinkle in His eyes when we laugh together from the current distance.

We are all better humans when we have some reve-lation of who we are because of Christ. Your experience finding your identity doesn't need to look like mine; it will be unique to you, your experience, and your purpose. After finding the basis of identity in a personal relationship with Christ, we can go further into the fulfilling experience of knowing who we were made to be specifically.

Discovering our identity is not about what we do but who we are. The root word for "are" is actually the verb "be." To get the point across a little more clearly, I like to take the phrase back to its roots: **It's not what we do, it's who we be.** One almost has to use bad grammar to get this point across because we don't want to start adding auxiliary verbs like *could* or *should*. When we do something, add-ing "could" suggests we are hopelessly not there yet, and "should" suggests there is more we need to "do" to get there. Instead, we need to make a discovery of who we *be*.

Personal Reflections

Before the Date

As you take your young adult on this series of dates, we will cover various subjects like giftings, personality, Love Languages™, and life experiences—all things that shape their unique identity among all the humans on earth. Listen to how your child looks at themselves and see how you can encourage and stabilize their view of who they are as a person uniquely designed by God and, if saved, a citizen of Heaven. As Christians, we should be exchanging our reputation for Christ's identity and our goals in life for His purposes. Who we *be* does not change in Heaven's view, no matter how people treat us or what circumstances surround us. Reassure your young adult that their worth is not measured in how they appear or what they do, but their value comes from the high ransom Jesus paid for their soul.

Some inspiring examples of that would be Stephen the first martyr, Dwight L. Moody, Dietrich Bonhoeffer, Corrie ten Boom, Elizabeth Elliot, and Nicki Cruz to mention a few. They all became born-again believers and were therefore justified by faith, called, and chosen to show and share Christ's love. The commission and purpose never changed, but the environments, pressures, needs, responses, challenges, details, and support around them sure did. Jesus stayed there for them always as He does for us.

These questions will be about whether both the positive and negative thoughts your adult feels are true about himself or herself, and we pray you can speak truth and perception into their perspective. You can make such a huge difference by giving another view and precious words of encouragement if they have doubts and fears about who they "be."

Active

Adventurous

Alert

Animated

Artistic

Authentic

Bossy

Blunt

Calm

Caring

Cool

Consistent

Courageous

Crafty

Creative

Daring

Dependable

Dependent

Detailed

Determined

Distracted

Dreamer

Dynamic

Earnest

Easygoing

Energetic

Extrovert

Flexible

Focused

Forceful

Forgetful

Forgiving

Fun

Gentle

Gracious

Happy

Helpful

Honest

Independent

Inspiring

Insightful

Intelligent

Introvert

Inventor

Kind

Leader

Loner

Loving

Loyal

Mature

Merciful

Moody

Motivator

Musical

Outgoing

Poetic

Reliable

Researcher

Reserved

Self-confident

Self-conscious

Sense of Humor

Sensitive

Serious

Serving

Sincere

Suspicious

Sporadic

Studious

Thoughtful

Thrifty

Tolerant

Trustworthy

Polite

Social

Silly

Undecided

Understanding

Warm

Wise

Visionary

Date Questions

Offense Check: Is there anything in your heart that I do, have done, or have not done in the past that irritated, belittled, hurt, shamed, angered, or let you down that might hinder you from trusting me and opening up on our date today?

1. What five adjectives would describe you when you are free to "be" who you just naturally are? Use the examples on the side of the page to help you think of your own.

    ____

    ____

    ____

    ____

    ____

2. What 3 characteristics can you "be" with a little more effort on your part?

    ____

    ____

    ____

3. What greater virtues and attributes do you think God is calling you to lately?

    ____

    ____

4. The God who created us and the Lord who suffered to buy our soul back knows and loves us more than ourselves or any human. That is why in His Word it encourages us in I Corinthians 10:12 that comparing ourselves among ourselves is not wise. As humans, we tend to still do it. Identity is how I view myself. Image is how I hope to portray myself. Reputation is how others view me. Are any of these thought habits or negative identity lies you have been feeling are true that we could discuss?

5. I am usually more ____________ than others around me.

6. I consider myself a pretty ______________ person.

7. I tend to ________________ when it comes to crowds.

8. No one seems to really ____________ me.

9. I feel like most people think I am __________________.

10. I tend to ____________________________ when I am with others.

11. People don't tend to ____ me.

12. I tend to think God sees me as

    ______________________________.

13. I tend to think God wants me to ____________________ more.

14. I consider myself viewed as ____________ and somewhat ________.

15. The negative thoughts I battle with the most are ________________.

16. Of the unchangeables in my life such as what time, era, and which geographical place and parents I was born into, I have the hardest time thanking God for ______________.

17. I am very grateful and like these three things about myself.

____

____

____

Closing Question

Now I am also open if there're any questions you've been wanting to ask me.

Adult Child's Prayer Sample

Thank you, Father, for allowing me to grow up into a young (man or woman) and for placing me into the home of ______________ in the year of ______. You have seen all the good and hard in my growing-up years. Please keep showing me how you look at me putting totally aside what anyone else in the world thinks of me or how I am treated. I ask you, Lord, to show me where the negative feelings "that I am ______ and ______ and sometimes even ______" originated so I can be healed from them.

Help me seek you all the days of my life for wisdom, and your identity and purpose for me! In Jesus's name, Amen.

Schedule

Take time to look at your next month's schedule, discuss with your child the next possible date, and pencil it in the index calendar as well as your planner or phone calendar.

Responses to Remember

Home

Date 3:
Maintaining a
Clear Conscience

Attraction Transaction

Love at first sight seems perfectly reasonable to an ambitious twelve-year-old. One yawning Sunday morning, the wooden church bench creaked as her blond head leaned over to the friend beside her. "*Who* is the raven-haired boy?!" she whispered as emphatically as the hushed tones allowed. It may have only been her sixth grade year, but she was instantly attracted to the newcomer who had just taken his seat.

This ambitious twelve-year-old was unaware of what her personal Maker knew. She would eventually meet and get acquainted with this raven-haired boy she wanted to love at first sight. She has no bragging rights to being a discreet and virtuous woman who waited in faith for God to bring her a husband in His time. The raven-haired boy responded to her adoration and pursued any chance to be around her until she was considered old enough to date. Whether in their earlier secret rendezvous or after they were enjoying an actual dating relationship, the fact that they had no connection or relationship with God affected how they experienced the next four years. They were living for themselves.

What my heart does rejoice in is how, during the four

years that they were getting to know each other, God used circumstances and His Spirit to draw them both to Himself for salvation. They unknowingly both responded during the same week, apart from each other.

In the privacy of their rooms, they desperately surrendered every area of their life and asked for cleansing of their past, engaging in the gracious exchange of the Spirit's peace and affirmation for their guilt and shame. Having dated four years with no confession of faith, they now experienced a new level of respect and sacredness in their fifth year of dating as new Christians. The blond girl, now a woman, walked down her wedding aisle to enter a covenant with God and her handsome love-at-first-sight, feeling very new and whole.

Our Story

I don't how your story goes, but the one above is ours. We have been telling our children from day one the mistakes we made and regret, with the goal to create a trusting, safe culture of complete honesty and openness in our home.

The degree of transparency and accountability we live with as parents will also be the degree by which our children will be open and accountable to us. As leaders, my husband and I try to not ask our children, employees, fellow church members, or disciples to apply principles we have not applied to ourselves first.

Before the Date

Are there things you have done in your life that you have not confessed to your spouse or children that bother your conscience?

The proper process is important for it to be a positive conversation and not adding sorrow or unnecessary visuals. Generally, it is best to just call your sin what the Bible calls it, without including names of other people involved. If they ask, it is good to give enough answers for them to picture your state of mind during that period of your life or to picture why you may have given in to temptation while excluding hurtful or unnecessary details. One of the goals of sharing is to become as honest and transparent with your child as you hope for your child to be with you. Only vulnerable, honest leaders have vulnerable, honest followers that remain feeling safe to relate in that way.

Another reason to share your unpleasant past is for young adult children to recognize the principles you violated and the natural reaping of consequences you have borne, in hopes that they try to avoid those same mistakes. While doing so, it is always best if you can share just enough for them to remember the story but no more details than necessary to avoid detailed, shameful visuals you and them would rather not have of you.

The admonishment that the Apostle John wrote on this subject in I John 3:20–24 gives us guidance to whether we truly are clear before God and between mankind or if we are living in condemnation ourselves.

This date's goal is to be a very gentle and safe friend who practices the art of listening well. If your young adult child doesn't seem to have anything to confess, think the best and go on to fun questions. If they have hard things to confess that you feel let down by, don't act shocked, smile understandingly, remember who you were at their age, and take it as a challenge to up your quality of adult friendship with them.

Date Questions

Offense Check: Is there anything in your heart that I do, have done, or have not done in the past that irritated, belittled, hurt, shamed, angered, or let you down that might hinder you from trusting me and opening up on our date today?

1. What is the last movie or media video you watched, and what would be a new food you would love for us to try to make at home?

2. What is one of the biggest stresses or fears you are processing lately?

3. Who are the closest friends you have of the opposite gender, and how open are you with each other?

4. What are two things you have a hard time forgiving and forgetting that someone did to you?

5. Where are most of your friends at with smoking, drinking, and drugs, and what forms, if any, have you tried?

6. How is it going as you try to maintain integrity in your viewing and communicating?

7. Have you ever had anyone threaten you into promising secrecy for something that bothers you at times?

8. Is masturbation or viewing inappropriate media an open and honest subject discussed among your friends, or do you personally battle it alone?

9. Do you have peace about all your shared texting and media pictures, conversations, or Snaps with friends?

10. Before we come to prayer and commit your current experiences and life challenges to the Lord, is there anything else in the past or currently that hinders you being able to walk in a totally clear conscience?

Closing Question

Now I am also open if there're any questions you've been wanting to ask me.

Spoken Blessing

I appreciate your honesty and openness and hope I can walk beside you, growing through the trials and celebrating the triumphs of life's seasons.

Prayer: I pray, Lord, you would always keep a ring of fire or Heavenly angels to protect (name) _____________, and I ask that (he or she) would be filled with the Holy Spirit according to (his or her) seeking you, to empower (her or him) to keep discerning wisely and know which battles to fight and where to surrender to your will and ways.

Schedule

Take time to look at your next month's schedule, discuss with your child the next possible date, and pencil it in the index calendar as well as your planner or phone calendar.

Responses to Remember

Skills to Steward

Our Story

I sighed heavenward, breathing a prayer for wisdom as I realized that this child of mine, although a good reader, could pass a spelling test one day and completely forget how to spell the words a week later. I never felt more fulfilled as a mother than when I was pregnant, breastfeeding, homeschooling, or carrying out one of our established family traditions. But feeling responsible to figure out how to meet a significant learning challenge for one of my children? Not so much.

After researching the symptoms and tendencies of a learning style, I realized my daughter had some dyslexic tendencies. I knew certain subjects would require individual attention and assistance to help her get through without feeling inadequate. I came up with some ideas that might help, purchased an additional program, and changed curriculum for that subject. I remember telling her that I refuse to put a certain label on her. While we acknowledged that it may take extra effort to succeed in specific assignments, it was no detriment to fulfilling God's calling in her life. My goal was to continue speaking into her and drawing out the creative writing and communication skills that I saw, in spite of the dyslexic tendencies in phonics.

During this same season, I was encouraged by a good friend to take in Carol Kent's "Speak Up" conference since God was opening up doors for me to speak to women. It was very helpful in learning to prepare a short speech and presenting it to total strangers, who had to do the same. We then scored each other, evaluating different areas of the presentation. Another such conference is IMPAC Communication Conference founded by Daryl Weaver and Rick Rhodes. The second time I went, I invited my daughter to join me at the "Speak Up" conference, and we took the writing sessions together to gain tips in both beginning and continuing our writing project goals.

Today, this daughter who struggled in phonics is an author of her own book called *Daughter*, a helpful conversation about the effects of our relationships with our dads. She has continual opportunities for writing, speaking, and other avenues of teaching and discipleship. I am currently grateful to have her wonderful input on this writing project as an author who has gone before me.

Your Story

If you see communication skills and a passion and authority to teach or share within your young adult, encourage them to become equipped for future opportunities God might open up. I had all my children take a public speaking course in high school because we all have a story and will probably have the opportunity to share it at some point.

When college, travel, and taking time off from work is not an option, there are many books, online webinars, podcasts, and YouTube channels in your young adult's areas of interest that are often free of charge. Our children took that self-education route instead of attending college in many fields such as photography, musical instruments, recording studios, sound equipment, voice, business, leadership, mechanics, and many other subjects.

The value and far-reaching fruits of encouraging our children to develop as many skills as possible while they are young, before they have jobs or become parents, is often underestimated because of our survival mentality during their adolescence. If you feel you didn't invest in their skills when your children were younger, there is no time like the present to start! Even adult children need the enrichment of parents who speak life, value, and belief into their lives. We have seen many platforms for discipleship and influence open up for people who are diligent to become excellent in a field, especially when they start while they are still young.

Personal Reflections

On This Date

I hope you can focus on what this young adult is good at and what jobs or opportunities bring them alive. Maybe you could ask them what they would like to add to their skill set if they had the time and consider how you can help make that happen. Look into any input or further training they could take in or a certain skill they can use for income or ministry in the future. Proverbs 18:16 reads, "A man's gift maketh room for him and bringeth him before great men" (KJV).

Date Questions

Offense Check: Is there anything in your heart that I do, have done, or have not done in the past that irritated, belittled, hurt, shamed, angered, or let you down that might hinder you from trusting me and opening up on our date today?

1. What is something new you learned or enjoyed reading about lately?

2. Is there a certain job, business vision, investment, or invention you have thought about that you would consider pursuing if it were possible?

3. Is there any skill, volunteer position, or service you would be passionate about getting involved with if finances were not an obstacle?

4. Have you considered investing time in furthering your knowledge in any of the arts like drama, speaking, voice lessons, music, sketching, journaling, writing, poetry, investing, painting, architectural design, sewing, needlework, or macramé?

5. Would you buy a little old house with land for a fixer-upper, a new ready-made tiny house, or a city apartment?

6. If you and I would decide to fly somewhere for a few days, where would you want to go?

7. Do you have any updating and home improvement ideas for us that would make a big difference for all of us living here as well as for hosting people?

8. Is one of these projects something you would gladly take charge of or love to assist in if we went through it?

9. If you had time and money to pursue further studies, education, or experiential training, what field would you be drawn to?

10. What is a position you would be honored to serve in or on a committee you would enjoy being on at your school, church, or in our community?

Closing Question

Now I am also open if there're any questions you've been wanting to ask me.

Spoken Blessing

Bless your adult for any skills they have been acquiring or working on no matter how insignificant or unproductive that skill may seem to you. Speak encouragement about things they are taking time to learn or work they are willing to do, though it may be mundane and not earn much money. If you suggest a new skill or job you would consider for them, make sure you state it with "I have thought of this and think you could accomplish or be successful in this, but I don't know if you have ever given it thought or could get excited about it?" Avoid pushing your goals and ideas of success upon them, but rather speak faith into them for purposeful pursuits.

Schedule

Take time to look at your next month's schedule, discuss with your child the next possible date, and pencil it in the index calendar as well as your planner or phone calendar.

Responses to Remember

Date 5:
Life Partner

My husband wrapped the soft blanket around us as we snuggled into an oversized wicker egg chair, side by side, with our low-calorie drinks and low-carb munchies as weight-watching people do in their fifties. We were settling in for our own little "us time" like empty nesters can, even though we have four adult children still abiding in rooms in our house. Between their working and socializing, we feel like we get the nightly benefit of empty nesters with the bonus of young adults who still come home for us to love on and talk to.

Serving on our church leadership team, we needed to preview some marriage DVD sets to prepare for the marriage retreat later that summer. We watched one of Tommy Nelson's sessions on Song of Solomon for anyone aspiring to date. He presented the idea of an immigrant friend who moved over here and was aghast at how barbaric our western practices were to start dating based on attraction instead of our parents making a rational decision about who would make a quality lifetime partner for us.

In their world, the prearranged couple trusts the romance will follow after they carry out their mutually committed love and care for each other.

How true that rings for my husband's and my original interest being based on physical attraction. We were lacking the mature depth and quality conversations that we should have had during our first four years of dating. If we had understood a few more concepts back then, it would have made a difference in our decisions and actions

I didn't understand that if I am not secure in my identity as an individual, without a partner, then I won't be secure once I have one either.

There is a balance to practically evaluating character and actually desiring and enjoying being with someone. We have walked with our children and supported not continuing relationships when they had wonderful qualities and character but were lacking attraction or enjoyment in each other's company. Unless you live in an area lacking opportunities to marry in the same faith, we would say: character plus attraction equals a good candidate for a life partner.

If you married without the feelings, God can bring, add, or resurrect them when you are open and willing to exercise unconditional love and tenderness.

Here are twelve characteristics God has been cultivating in our lives that have been vital to a healthy marriage for us. We thank God we are still very attracted to each other after thirty years of marriage!

1. Being willing to listen well, without interrupting or defending ourselves. Not leaving the scene in anger when we don't feel encouraged or get our preference.

2. Being respectful and valuing the other person enough to not violate their purity for our own lust before marriage.
3. Being an adult who can be trusted to assist in raising up the next generation and pass on a legacy of faith.
4. Being able to apply self-discipline in all areas of our life for the good of ourselves and others.
5. Being willing to honor even those we disagree with.
6. Being teachable and open to look at constructive criticism in spite of the faults or attitude of the person from whom they came.
7. Placing God before our own selfish desires while having some understanding of who He created us to be.
8. Honoring all authorities that are placed over us and living with a healthy fear of God, acknowledging the ever-true, ongoing consequences of reaping what you sow.
9. Believing in the infallibility of the Word of God.
10. Not being afraid of hard work, trials, and heart-to-heart, deep conversations.
11. Being humble enough to admit being wrong and apologizing.
12. Choosing gratitude and praise when times get tough.

Personal Reflections

On This Date

You will want to listen to your young adult child first, and then if it seems fitting and your child is still interested, you can watch the QR code on testimonies from our young adult children. They will share some of their personal learning experiences in dating and courting. If they seem to welcome further discussion, you could ask for their feedback on the twelve characteristics listed above after you've heard them out on the other first ten date questions.

Date Questions

Offense Check: Is there anything in your heart that I do, have done, or have not done in the past that irritated, belittled, hurt, shamed, angered, or let you down that might hinder you from trusting me and opening up on our date today?

1. What is a personality or type of person you tend to be attracted to?

2. What are a few skills and spiritual gifts you lack that might be helpful in a life partner to balance your home and calling?

3. What are some deal breakers for you when you consider dating someone?

4. What are a few characteristics that tend to really irritate or make you draw away from considering getting to know someone for a life partner?

5. What is a way of thinking in your generation of youth that burdens you?

6. What are some skin types, hair tones or textures, dress styles, or virtues you appreciate and find refreshing and pleasing in the opposite gender?

7. Have you taken a test or know what your personality type would be described as in any of these or other studies? Enneagram (9 personality types), Myers Briggs (16 personality types), Big Five Assessment, Career Profile, Workplace DISC Test, etc.

8. What are the weaknesses or tendencies with those personalities that you need to notice and work on, for your own sake as well as how it affects others?

9. Are there personalities that are not you at all but could be a fun or good fit for your life partner?

10. What are some biblical principles that are important for you to see lived out in a life partner as well as applied in your marriage and home?

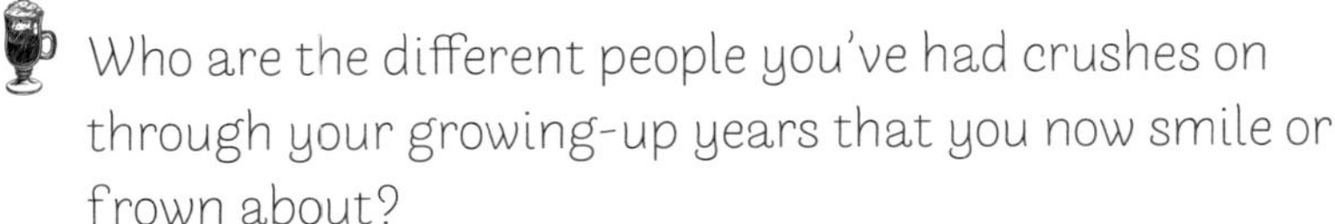 Who are the different people you've had crushes on through your growing-up years that you now smile or frown about?

Closing Question

Now I am also open if there're any questions you've been wanting to ask me.

Spoken Blessing

Speak into this young adult the type of life partner you are believing and praying for them and any specific characteristics or values you believe would be expedient to their well-being if God also sees it as important.

Schedule

Take time to look at your next month's schedule, discuss with your child the next possible date, and pencil it in the index calendar as well as your planner or phone calendar.

Responses to Remember

Discovering Their Spiritual Gift

Turning right on Howard Gap Road, my husband and I feasted our eyes on that familiar, almost-home view of the weathered, two-story barn out in the middle of the manicured field. A fresh stream bordered one side, and a sequential row of tall pines lined the road on the other. The setting sun formed an ever-changing hue of blue and green on the hardwoods covering our Blue Ridge Mountains in the horizon. We both spotted the elderly landowner once again raking the fresh layers of mowed grass with his two faithful German shepherds in tow.

I mentioned that I have considered stopping to encourage him in appreciation for how beautifully he keeps his field. It is a feast for the eyes of everyone who drives by there daily. My husband started chuckling to himself, to which I inquired how he would find that thought humorous. He explained that he had also thought of stopping and talking to the man but with a different goal for his approach. Curious, I asked what his thought had been. He said he wants to inquire if it is not an idol to this man, considering the amount of time and resources he invests in a grassy field.

Which one of us was in tune with the Holy Spirit? Which

one of us was hearing and walking with God? Do you and your close ones ever run into this question with differences of views on circumstances and events when dissecting a situation or teaching content?

Perhaps God has placed gift-sized portions of his characteristics into individuals, showing glimpses of who He is and what He does. Perhaps He kindly downloads them into people who believe in His Son as their personal Sacrificial Lamb for the remission of their sins. And maybe we don't always have the full picture, which can lead to conflicts unless we are willing to hear each other and lean into grace.

Studying what the different gifts are called and what their purposes, functions, and human weakness or imbalance tend to be can help us use them more effectively. It is also helpful to recognize how we need other believers' perspectives to balance out all the views God might have of one situation or purpose in His Kingdom.

After thirty years of marriage, we have come to accept, appreciate, and even celebrate our different views and giftings. My husband's motivational gift for all the others he functions in would seem to be evangelism, or making sure everyone's life is ready for eternity. He functions in the gifts of discernment, prophecy, apostleship, and administration to carry out that goal as well. My motivational gift is exhortation, or assisting people to find their full potential in their Maker while here on earth and for all eternity. I function in mercy, teaching, serving, and intercession to carry that out.

We have five adult children and have had fun discovering more of who God made them to be and what gifts He has given them to carry out in love. I had our children read and fill out a book called *Life Purpose Planner* when they were preteens and then again in high school. It was exciting to see how the answers remained similar yet they became clearer as time went on. This study of spiritual gifts is closely related to, and can be paired well with, learning your life message. They are distinctive but paired. Spiritual gifts are given freely without any merit, while your life message comes with the price you have paid with your life. Your life message is formed and birthed through the hard and great things you have experienced, and the spiritual gifts you have been granted will be used to encourage, edify, and build up others *through* your life message.

My husband had the tradition of printing out and framing a father's blessing for each of our children when they graduated from high school. Included in it, he would mention the gifts and talents he sees in their life already and what he envisions them carrying out for God's kingdom.

The way your children are currently exercising their gifts will change as seasons change and as they are given weightier assignments after faithfulness in smaller ones. May God give you wisdom as a mentor to study and encourage your young adult. If they do not yet know what their gifts are, consider doing an online test or study to find out. Not knowing our gifts can hinder us from fully appreciating the natural skill responsibility God has given us to serve our families, churches, communities, and the world. Knowing their gifts and the current assignments for exercising them can make all the difference in how a person spends their time and resources.

Whenever you exercise a gift that the Holy Spirit empowers, you receive something too. In fact, you often receive more than the recipients as God's power and grace flows through you for others! May your time together today bring your young adult child closer to experiencing the fulfillment of being all that he or she can be for their Maker's glory.

Personal Reflections

Date Questions

Offense Check: Is there anything in your heart that I do, have done, or have not done in the past that irritated, belittled, hurt, shamed, angered, or let you down that might hinder you from trusting me and opening up on our date today?

1. Before we get into discussing this subject, do you already have an idea of a few of the spiritual gifts you have been given?

2. What are some ways you see God currently using those gifts through you to encourage or help others?

3. Would you rather teach a class, serve refreshments, surprise someone with a gift, write encouraging words in a card, offer a back rub, or organize a small group to meet weekly?

4. If you were to visit a sick person in the hospital, how would you try to encourage them?

5. By offering advice on what to do to get better

6. By offering to take care of their pets or things at the house while they are gone

7. By encouraging them that God is with them in this

8. By preparing a nice gift and card or money for them

9. By rubbing their stiff muscles

10. By listening as they share the story of their accident

11. What would be a dream ministry title for you to be known as?

12. What do you usually see as a need in your church that is not happening enough?

13. What should Christians do more to help the community?

14. What type of ways do you feel nudged by the Holy Spirit to start before practically being the change you want to see in the world?

15. How do you see yourself being an asset to your home, church, or community?

16. What gifts are you lacking that might help balance out your home and ministry if God would give those gifts in your life partner?

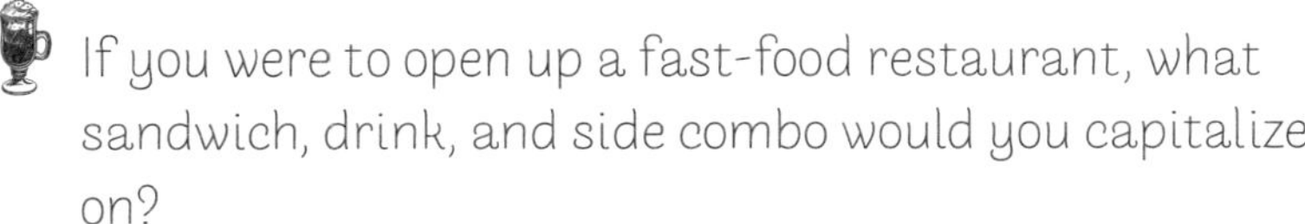 If you were to open up a fast-food restaurant, what sandwich, drink, and side combo would you capitalize on?

Closing Question

Now I am also open if there're any questions you've been wanting to ask me.

Spoken Blessing

Lay hands on and pray over your young adult. Confirm and call to life all the gifts of the Spirit that He wants to impart and anoint them with in order for them to be effective and bring forth much fruit in the Kingdom of God. Add anything else God gives you faith for or brings to your mind.

Schedule

Take time to look at your next month's schedule, discuss with your child the next possible date, and pencil it in the index calendar as well as your planner or phone calendar.

Responses to Remember

Date 7:

Personalities

The four van doors slamming broke the dark night's hush. Seven of us bounded up three narrow steps, putting us all in the front of our forty-foot motor home. Most of us were eager to be the first to claim the bathroom and then hit our bunks. While one was brushing their teeth, another grabbed an umbrella for a quick walk to enjoy the soft, lingering rain and pour out her heart to God under the rising moon.

The third born decided that the food served at the place of fellowship had not quite been satisfactory and planned to top it off with a bowl of cereal with the big gallon jar of fresh farm milk someone gave us. As he lifted the gallon jar to place it on the kitchen counter, the jar's side hit the solid edge. Clear glass and all the white liquid inside burst into a rushing river. Little pieces of glass and droplets of milk flowed in every direction of that narrow, congested room.

Gasps and groans followed the crashing, and a teenage head popped out of the bathroom, toothbrush dangling from his mouth. He quickly leaped for towels and jumped in with the two brothers who were grasping for anything to sop up the liquid. My husband was scrambling to keep the milk from running into the couch, carpet, and the camper's slide out. The milk prevailed, as did our desperation in imagining the rotting smells to come.

I ushered our youngest daughter onto the couch immediately, instructing her, "Stay off the floor so you don't cut your feet!" Turning, I frantically exclaimed that the milk was running down onto the dry, clean curtain covering the fourth bunk we built under the sink. Already, the boy who dropped the jar was feeling ashamed, and my husband hushed me. The turmoil remained, turning inward.

You can imagine the tension as we all silently tried to do our best to help clean and avoid a future rotten-dairy smell in our home on the road. All the while each of us silently thinking of the hurt felt or observed by another in our stressed reactions. My family journal from the time describes the feeling in the room, saying, "It was a thirty-minute, tedious, 'stressfully quiet' process." Meanwhile the older daughter had no idea the drama she had escaped by choosing to take a tranquil evening walk.

It was past midnight until we had heard out and apologized to the child who had felt blamed, the child who felt yelled at, as well as the two innocent helpful brothers that felt the tension caused by our words. Last, my husband and I got the exchanges between us talked out and forgiven and tried to get some much-needed sleep. Beautifully, though, the last sentence in that journal entry tells of the *rhema* God gave me from His Word the next morning for the personal woes in my heart at the time, even before the milk spilled.

Can you picture each character and personality in your home and what they all bring that makes you laugh and cry at the same time? What good cultural changes might this child's good or challenging attributes have brought into your lifestyle?

Our oldest is a peacemaker and maybe agrees with too many people but has no enemies. He would have kindly assisted all he could, comforted the offended, and calmed the stressed that night. Then the oldest daughter on the umbrella walk feels things deeply and is a sensitive soul, which created some trials but more joys for us parents. We noticed when she moved away, we didn't make as much time for intentional group talks and celebratory events, which used to connect our hearts and add meaningful memories together.

Our upbringing also plays into how our personality is actually lived out. For instance, my family culture was more unpredictable, overextending, spontaneous, and reactionary. My husband's family culture was calm, organized, and void of surprises or stress whenever possible.

In my upbringing, I remember distinctly a sharp-tongued negative reaction to us children if we broke any precious dishes. I was determined that my children would never feel that a dish was more important than they were. But as you can see, in the heat of the moment of the spilled milk, I still focused on the dry-cleaned bunk curtain over the feelings of my son, and my husband cringed.

Thankfully, children are very forgiving when we acknowledge the hurt we inflicted. I am reminded of how this affected me in my view of the value system in our home. If us parents never apologize, and our grown children don't recognize and process it in a healthy way, they may carry hurt as a pain trigger point and identity problem unaware.

Picture the differences between you and your spouse and be motivated. You can help your children see and work on their strengths and weaknesses so their spouse and employers won't need to do as much of this for them. When you love someone, you will be kinder in how you approach constructive criticism than the average person they run into in their world.

Listening to DISC, Enneagram, or other personalities teaching podcasts can really help your child more fully see their strengths and when to watch for pitfalls or destructive behavior that mar the great personality they were given.

Enjoy studying your young adult, remaining curious and grateful. As their mentor and friend on this date, try not to focus so much on what they do but who they are.

Personal Reflections

Date Questions

Offense Check: Is there anything in your heart that I do, have done, or have not done in the past that irritated, belittled, hurt, shamed, angered, or let you down that might hinder you from trusting me and opening up on our date today?

1. Are you an extrovert who likes to be with people in order to chill or more of an introvert who prefers to just be alone in order to relax and be refreshed?

2. Do you prefer to be in charge of a project, or would you rather serve the leader well to get the goals accomplished?

3. What lack of character in others really gets your goat?

4. What frustrates you most in a group project?

5. Do you consider yourself more of a visionary, server, leader, encourager, or teacher?

6. Do you tend to focus more on what's happening currently in your life or plan and dream about the future?

7. Do you get more accomplished when you are all alone and organized or under pressure surrounded by people?

8. What would be your idea of a wonderful day off?

9. How has your birth order in the family affected you positively and negatively?

10. What personality type do you tend to think would be helpful or fun to have in a life partner to stand with you in support yet bring something you are not naturally?

 Who would be someone you'd enjoy seeing in concert?

Closing Question:

Now I am also open if there're any questions you've been wanting to ask me.

Spoken Blessing

I bless you for what your personality brings to our home and family and the people around you and for who you are naturally when people let you feel safe to be yourself. I want to be one of those who welcomes the real you and appreciates and celebrates how you were designed by our Maker. I want to walk with you as we become aware of the weaknesses that are your personality's tendencies, giving grace and encouragement to overcome. I want you to feel free to be yourself with us.

Responses to Remember

Discovering Their Life Mission

I sat beside my husband on the loveseat as the noon sun from the picture window warmed our little living room. He had just returned from a requested mystery meeting with the field representative of an evangelistic ministry. He excitedly filled me in on why the gentleman had wanted to meet with him: to replace this man's position as field representative since he felt called to start a counseling ministry with his wife. It would include a lot of administrative tasks as the forerunner for the itinerant evangelist and a relocation to base out of North Carolina.

My husband sighed as he described to me the perplexity of his dilemma. After serving in prison care ministry, we had moved back to our home area, and my husband was voted in as one of three candidates for a third pastoral role in our church. This man I loved had sensed and responded to a personal call to the Great Commission before we were married. His spiritual gifts included evangelism. He began to feel a very strong urge to preach. Well, he was not the one out of the three licensed at that time. Unbeknown to us, he would be ordained as an itinerant evangelist by that same congregation several years later.

As my husband sat across from me that Saturday morning on the loveseat listing the job descriptions, he looked a bit let down. He had no desire to fill those roles in the office or field. These responsibilities did not replicate his desire to preach the gospel and evangelize the lost at all. It seemed a confusing let down because of how excited he would be to work for the fiery evangelist of that ministry whom he admired.

As he shared his dilemma with me, I saw the word picture of a ladder. I sensed my husband was supposed to start at the bottom of the ladder and be faithful to serve the evangelistic ministry as a young disciple. God would promote him rung by rung to his fulfillment and calling as he was obedient and served his authorities in honor.

He felt the grace and calling to say yes in spite of the less attractive responsibilities he was given. We agreed in faith that it was where God wanted us to serve at the time.

Often men and women of God experience the death of a vision, or a wilderness, like Moses and Joseph did in the Old Testament. During this time, hopefully any self-performance and personal agenda are gently broken and replaced with surrender. Good qualities of character build so that when the vision does come to pass, it is in God's way and timing. Are we humble enough to give Him all the glory as we serve His purpose?

The picture I had of that ladder is exactly what happened to my husband. Another part of his wilderness, and test of laying down the vision, came during the first and second rung of that ladder. With God's grace to follow His principles of honoring authorities, and my constant encouragement, my husband passed one test after the other on the road of obedience and humility. God saw and knew his difficult circumstances, and God was faithful to fulfill the vision he gave my husband years earlier.

After he had received much strength and brokenness in the secret closet of worship and prayer, God opened so many doors of opportunity for my husband to preach the gospel to his heart's fulfillment, with our authority's blessing, that he could not walk through them all. As I write two decades later, he is now on another rung as the executive director of the ministry and helping our grown children and other disciples see the importance of allowing "the death of the vision" journey to break and mold us in preparation for our high callings.

I personally have experienced this principle in my own visions and callings, and I hope that as you listen to any visions and dreams God may be placing on your young adult, you also can help them prepare for the wilderness before it comes. Those seasons are a great time of molding them into Kingdom Warriors fit for the King and His excellent ways.

Our calling never changes, but our assignments do. Nancy Ray explains this concept of calling versus assignment very well in her podcast called *Work and Play*. Referring to Ephesians 5, she says that "Our calling is to Jesus, but our assignments change during different seasons" (episode #131). She uses Elizabeth Elliot as an example. One of Elizabeth's assignments was to be the wife of Jim Elliot for a season, until he passed away. Later her assignment was to be the wife of two more husbands, but that whole time she was called to Jesus and the cause of the Gospel, whatever that looked like.

Once my husband had said yes to Jesus's Lordship, he was accepting the assignments God sent his way to train and equip him for weightier assignments down the road.

As he kept his eyes toward the more desirable assignment, he did many menial assignments faithfully while using and growing his skill sets for more excellence in future assignments.

After your adult son or daughter is done sharing goals, burdens, or visions they might sense, and you have listened without interrupting, prepare to speak your words of faith and blessing on any dreams or vision they have shared, that you could possibly endorse, even if they are different from what yours were for them. Don't be afraid to share any visions you see for their individual life if it is not with a selfish motive of your own personal gain or reputation. You as the parents can feel free to encourage your young adult in something you see as a valuable experience for them. You will want to be careful to discern whether there's any interest at all and be willing to lay it down if not.

Personal Reflections

Date Questions

Offense Check: Is there anything in your heart that I do, have done, or have not done in the past that irritated, belittled, hurt, shamed, angered, or let you down that might hinder you from trusting me and opening up on our date today?

1. What burdens you the most in our world today?

2. Have some creative solutions come to your mind to help solve that problem?

3. If someone gave you $500,000 to make a difference in the world, what would you do with it?

4. Who would you be most drawn to help and encourage? Why are you drawn to that group?
    - fatherless children
    - poor or homeless people
    - missionaries or pastors' families
    - emergency or medical workers
    - political people
    - unbelievers
    - inmates
    - inner-city kids
    - gangs
    - abused children
    - orphans
    - trafficked individuals
    - people suffering from substance abuse and addictions

- transgender people
- people with abortion trauma
- handicapped people
- elderly people
- sick people
- business people
- people in other religions or cults
- high school or college students
- agnostic or atheistic people

5. If you could earn a title or position that names some- one who makes a difference in society, what would that title be?

6. Would you rather speak, sing, give gifts, serve, or pray with needy people?

7. If you could live out the quote "be the change you want to see in society," what would that look like?

8. If you could give the president, senators, governors, or mayors some advice to lead our country and communities, what would you say to them?

9. What would you want people to say about you at your funeral?

10. What's the biggest compliment you ever got or could get?

Closing Question

Now I am also open if there're any questions you've been wanting to ask me.

Spoken Blessing

I am excited about your future and believe God has great exploits He wants to do through you to encourage and impact individuals through your story and what you have been through. I pray you will continue to seek God's face and receive His grace to develop through perseverance added character and skills out of each trial you face and mountain you climb. May our Lord be pleased and glorified as you steward your body and health, money, time, talents, and resources as you continue your journey of faith.

Schedule

Take time to look at your next month's schedule, discuss with your child the next possible date, and pencil it in the index calendar as well as your planner or phone calendar.

Responses to Remember

Date 9:
Lies

One of my favorite moments of the morning used to be when my daughter would come upstairs and greet me with her humorously proper, "Good morning, Mother," and I would be entertained by whatever outfit she had put together for her day. I was adding a dab of coconut oil to my cast-iron pan when her eyes took a second look at me and asked, "Are you okay?" My grim, "I'm not, but I will be," led her to put her forenoon agenda aside and move in closer. She motioned for me to turn off the stove, implying cooking could wait, and invited me to her room, into the cozy chair across from her bed.

I welcomed her care and shared how it had begun the night before with a gift idea I had for my dad, who lived in another state. I presented the idea to my husband, and there my problems began. My husband has the gift of discerning motives and spirits. It can be so amazing and helpful—until it's exercised on me! He had seen through my attempts to please and win a heart-to-heart connection from my dad, whom I felt rejected by, and therefore he had little desire to endorse and finance my idea.

As usual, I was attempting to paint this story background for my listening daughter in as honest, unbiased, and honorable a way as I could toward my husband. I told her how we had tried to resolve the hurt and misunderstanding last night, lest "the sun go down upon our wrath," but it felt more like a Band-Aid on an infected wound for me by the next day.

Through my "misunderstood" filter, I believed my husband didn't understand or relate to how much I miss being with family members since we moved away over twenty years ago. I reacted out of another negative emotion filter of being uncared for, pinning his response as an insensitive husband to my unmet needs as the reason for our conflict.

This daughter had training in caring for the heart and getting to the root of lies, and was familiar with where to start with my heart. She asked me how I was feeling. I filled her in on all the ways that I miss the people that just get me and bring life and encouragement to my life that don't live close to us. She proceeded to ask me how that makes me feel. I filled her in on how plugging in where we live, while being gone a lot, as well as some differences in goals can leave me feeling like I won't ever be "one of" the original group of women in our church.

She followed that up with "Why do you feel that way?" To which I said I don't know, but I never feel like they actually like me for who I am without offering some service, which was another lie filter I had of being unaccepted. She asked why believing I was unaccepted made me feel lonely. She followed up by repeating to me, not that it is true, but does it *feel* true that you are misunderstood and unaccepted and therefore lonely? I said yes, and we presented these negative emotions to the Lord asking Him for revelation of where they originate from so I can renounce the lie revealed and receive God's revelation of opposing truth for it. If I could close that door that either I or someone else had opened to the enemy, I can then go on and experience healing from that filter in my life.

After many tears, and a pile of accumulated tissues, the Lord brought a memory to my mind. It was a group of teenage girls on bikes. Right away, I knew what the Lord was referring to and who that group was. In my neighborhood, church, school, and cousins, I felt accepted among peers growing up, but after I graduated eighth grade and got my high school diploma through GED classes, I needed to find new friends.

In this search, I would bike to girls' houses my age a mile or more away to work on new friendships. These friends all had established friendships with girls that had been each other's cousins, school friends, and neighbors all their lives, and they did not necessarily need another one. My attempts to establish an ongoing social life with these newfound friends that had welcomed me but never invited me to a future event started me on a journey of feeling rejected and unwanted or uninvited.

I am happy to say that after I wept and acknowledged the painful events of those years and how they had felt, committing the results of God to heal me, I no longer experience that filter of feeling uninvited by people like I used to! The lie does not feel real, and it seems all the people have changed their attitude around me, when in actuality, it was me who had changed.

Before the Date

This date is to validate negative emotions your child may have experienced, but not to cast blame or use names more than you have to. We only ask about these things so that we can face how they are affecting us currently and find grace to heal, not to blame others in the process. The question is never so much "who did it?" as "how can I find grace to forgive and not be hindered by the memory of it?"

My first goal for this date is that you as the mature adult can attempt to be an excellent listener that does not interrupt, downplay, diminish, or disagree with what your young adult says they have experienced or felt.

The second goal is for you and your date to write down or document in your phone the main three self-identity lies or negative emotions that the child seems to repeatedly experience and bring them before God in the closing prayer.

If you already know what area seems unhealthy, maybe you can talk to them about how you see them differently through your unoffended lens of faith and let them know how you would counteract the negative view with a positive one.

If you still really don't know what area they are struggling in after the specific questions on the date, you can extend this subject by planning another date and tap into the section in the index called "What Am I Afraid of?"

Personal Reflections

Date Questions

Offense Check: Is there anything in your heart that I do, have done, or have not done in the past that irritated, belittled, hurt, shamed, angered, or let you down that might hinder you from trusting me and opening up on our date today?

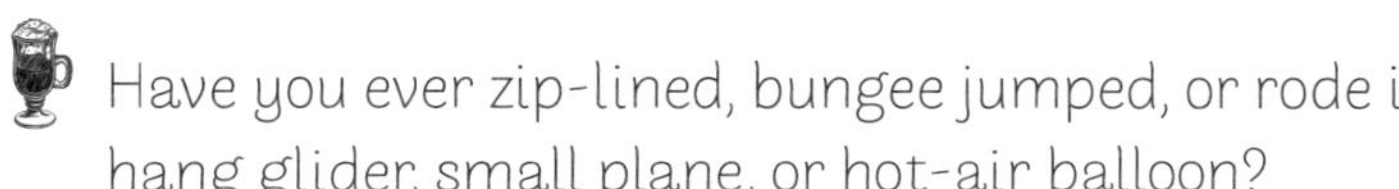 Have you ever zip-lined, bungee jumped, or rode in a hang glider, small plane, or hot-air balloon?

1. Has someone offended you in a way that you really feel like justice should be served?

2. Is there a time that one of us parents hurt your feelings or shut you down?

3. What is something that shuts you down quickly?

4. What settings do you try to avoid because it feels awkward or daunting? Why?

What famous person of the past or present would you enjoy meeting?

5. Is there someone who has said things that you have a hard time debunking your identity? Why?

6. What would you say is the most traumatic thing you've experienced, and how has that affected your thinking?

7. Do you consider yourself creative, talented, and wise? If not, why not?

8. Do you like the way God created you? What part is hard to embrace at times?

9. Are there certain circumstances that seem to bring more feelings of rejection than normal?

 What are your favorite places to shop, eat, and chill out right now?

10. Who do you feel most relaxed, safe, and able to be yourself with? Why?

Closing Question:

Now I am also open if there're any questions you've been wanting to ask me.

Prayer Suggestion for the Young Adult

If your young adult child has specific negative lies they believe about themselves, they may need a renewing of their mind in order to walk in faith in what is true.

Lord, I bring to you the things we talked about that are hard for me to forget.

1. The scenario where ________ said this and ______________ and I felt so ______.
2. Then also the time that ________________ when I was __________ and I ______________.
3. And, Lord, you know I want to forgive _________, but it still makes me feel so __________ when I think about that.
4. Please give me compassion and grace to forgive those once again who did not realize how they made me feel.
5. Jesus, I plead Your blood over these lies about who I am and the negative emotions I have and present the scars to you for healing. Please transform them into compassion for others.

6. I renounce these lies that I am _______________ and _______________ and accept Heaven's love and acceptance for me. I pray I can experience it as reality soon. I believe that I am worth very much because you gave your only Son to buy my soul back.

Spoken Blessing by Parent

I thank You, Father, for creating (name of child) _______________ and deciding which family and time era (he or she) would live in. We ask you to continue to reveal experiences in (his or her) childhood that have marred the original image of who (name of child) _______________ was intended to be. Please restore and make whole (his or her) soul so (he or she) can also see others the way you meant for (him or her) to view them.

Another good way to counteract the lies your young adult has believed is to show affirmation and love through their preferred Love Language™. Below is a link for them to take the test to determine what that is or read the book ***The 5 Love Languages™ for Singles*** by Gary Chapman. https://5lovelanguages.com/quizzes/love-language

Responses to Remember

Date 10:
Sacred Things

Parent Tip

When the mail arrived from Europe, my daughter carefully slit through the adhesive packaging, making sure no sharp end was inserted into the box's contents. She excitedly lifted the flaps to reveal ivory folds of soft but weighty crocheted lace that would overlay the bridal gown she had designed. After a lovely day in the city trying on and observing different gowns, fabrics, patterns, laces, and shades of white, and comparing online pricing, the bride had chosen this European lace for her wedding dress.

Although she was designing her own wedding dress, and we were both seamstresses, we agreed we would prefer to not have the pressure of sewing it during her short, three-month engagement. We found a good seamstress two and a half hours away, which meant she would be making weekly trips to try on the dress. Although I was still homeschooling our youngest high schooler, I knew right away that good could come out of this and told my oldest daughter I would be glad to drive with her every week. There was a lot on my plate, but it was a great time for us to connect and stay in communication, savoring our last weeks with her in our home and state.

Those five hours together for four weeks turned out to be the biggest highlight and security for both of us. She caught up with her "bride to-do list" and phone calls in the first hour, and then we could discuss a wide variety of subjects pertaining to switching from twenty-five years of singlehood to married life and adjusting to the transition into a new state and community. We would discuss everything from human anatomy and honeymoon expectations to friends' first-year experiences and any engaged woman's dreams, qualms, and concerns. I gathered some of my books on anatomy and intimacy in marriage for some good references.

From elementary age on up, we had discussed avoiding too much emotional, spiritual, or physical connection with friends of the opposite gender. Now that our daughter was engaged, I could open the subject in more detail. As they dated, they had formed spiritual, intellectual, and emotional connections, and now they would take the further step of physical connection once married.

If you have been transparent with your children from young on up about private and reproductive subjects, these facts of life discussions don't need to be awkward. It is a privilege when you are one of the main people they are learning and getting perspective from. Notice that I said one of them? We are only kidding ourselves if we don't think they discuss this with their peers, even before they may be ready to experience dating or marriage. All of us were curious in our teens and twenties and felt much more comfortable discussing it with friends in our age group than grown-ups.

Unless we as parents invite them into these discussions safely through the years, without projecting shame or judgment, they will probably prefer the subject discussions to be with their youth mentors, coaches, or friends. I know a parent that was very disappointed when they made plans to have "the marriage night" talk with their child the week of the wedding, only to discover the child had all the needed conversations with young married friends and siblings long before and had no questions left for them.

Personal Reflections

Before the Date

Whether your adult is single, dating, engaged, or married, I hope you can gently tell them you would love to have an "adult-to-adult" conversation about their personal journey with physical desires. Discern if it is a good time for this type of conversation or if you have other unresolved conflicts or subjects that need to be addressed first.

If you haven't been as intentional and discussed a lot of personal things with your children as they grew up, you will probably want to acknowledge this as you try to open a conversation with your young adult about their private moral life.

Consider it as serious an event as you would if you were to approach an adult employee or church friend about something in their personal life or character. Think carefully about your timing, approach, and attitude.

We as parents always want to try to make our children feel valued and might need to ask if they feel safe in the conversation or uneasy or threatened.

Date Questions

Offense Check: Is there anything in your heart that I do, have done, or have not done in the past that irritated, belittled, hurt, shamed, angered, or let you down that might hinder you from trusting me and opening up on our date today?

Our QR code video conversation at the bottom of the page, done by a young doctor and his wife, may break the ice and help open the way for conversation if you want to use this first rather than afterward.

1. What are some subjects or areas of life where your view or opinion has changed as you have matured?

2. Have you made any new friends lately that have influenced or enhanced your thinking or goals about dating or marriage?

3. What are some of your goals in the area of a life partner?

    If you could take a trip to any state or country for a week, where would it be and why?

4. Have you been let down, hurt, offended, or felt violated by anyone of the opposite gender—in the past or lately?

5. How would you describe your goals morally, and how has it been to uphold them in this season of your life?

    Who's your favorite comedian, and what's their best line or story?

6. Which of your friends would you say is the best ac-countability or safe person for you to discuss morals with?

7. How is your generation and friend group viewing the subject of masturbation or porn or don't they discuss it?

8. Where do most of your generation, friends, and you stand on being a virgin when you marry?

9. Do you understand a female's cycle and which days she can conceive?

10. Do you have any questions concerning a female's eggs and a male's sperm and how God made the wonder of it all to be a beautiful way to bring babies into a family?

🍺 Have you ever seen a pregnancy test?

Closing Question

Now I am also open if there're any questions you've been wanting to ask me.

Spoken Blessing

I am grateful for your openness and time today. I am honored to be a person in your life that you trust to discuss a lot of subjects in your life. I pray you will hear, know, and heed God's leading in the very important subject of singlehood or choosing a life partner. God and I both want what is best for you and your future and want to be as involved in your big, life-altering choices as you welcome us to be. May you have the desire to take the high road when brought to a "Y" of choices or temptations. You have a specific calling, and I believe He will keep equipping you to fulfill that, no matter where you go or who you tend to compare your-self with. I like who you "be."

Responses to Remember

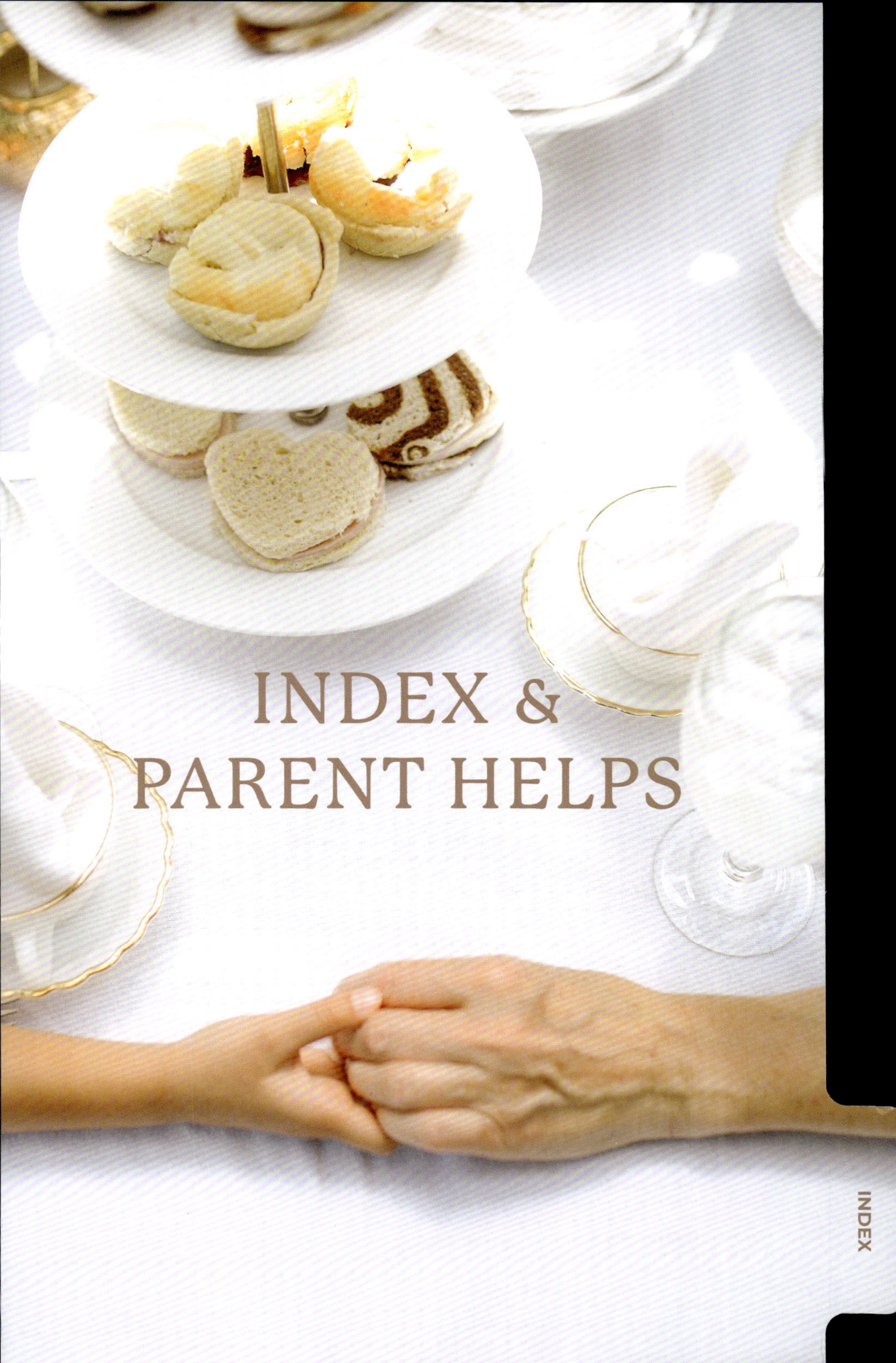

INDEX &
PARENT HELPS

Calendar Pages

The following calendar pages can be used to help plan future dates and track dates that have already taken place. This book can be used for more than one child and multiple initial boxes have been provided for each date which will allow you to record the dates you have completed with each child.

It's a date! Preschool: Ages 3-5

Setting forth your weekly or monthly goals.

Initials of Child

Date 1

Date 2

Date 3

Date 4

Date 5

Date 6

Date 7

Date 8

Date 9

Date 10

Memories & Goals

It's a date! Elementary: Ages 6-10

Setting forth your weekly or monthly goals.

Initials of Child

Date 1

Date 2

Date 3

Date 4

Date 5

Date 6

Date 7

Date 8

Date 9

Memories & Goals

It's a date! Middle School: Ages 11-14

Setting forth your weekly or monthly goals.

Initials of Child

Date 1

Date 2

Date 3

Date 4

Date 5

Date 6

Date 7

Date 8

Date 9

Date 10

Memories & Goals

It's a date! High School: Ages 15-17

Setting forth your weekly or monthly goals.

Initials of Child

Date 1

Date 2

Date 3

Date 4

Date 5

Date 6

Date 7

Date 8

Date 9

Date 10

Memories & Goals

It's a date! College or Career: Ages 19 & Up

Setting forth your weekly or monthly goals.

Initials of Child

Date 1

Date 2

Date 3

Date 4

Date 5

Date 6

Date 7

Date 8

Date 9

Date 10

Memories & Goals

Being a Good Listener

Do: Listen well, looking relaxed, with unfolded arms, a pleasant, kind, smiling face, and make eye contact while watching their face.

Don't:
- Interrupt
- Cross your arms, appearing guarded
- Crease your forehead or scowl when they are talking
- Disagree
- Become offended
- Defend yourself or others
- Glance at distractions close by

No matter how falsely accused you might feel by the information your child gives, resist the urge to interrupt. If the child has put walls up around their heart and can't trust you fully with honesty, it is your responsibility to figure out why.

You will want to ask pointed, specific questions and learn to really listen to begin bringing down any walls or barriers. You can figure out how the trust was broken and what it will look like for that trust to start being rebuilt.

Remember to be very patient with introverted or more private personalities that may not be as natural to verbalize and express what they are thinking. Try giving them a few examples of what type of responses you are looking for in order to help them learn to verbalize life experiences more specifically such as "Was your time today a letdown, a struggle, or a very fulfilling time, and why would you describe it that way?" We never want them to feel inadequate or awkward; we want to help them learn to express what they are experiencing.

Being More of an Asker

When our three sons were high-school age, for a few years they could all play on the same local rec basketball team. This made for great comradery, aiding smooth passes and buckets and causing lots of fan excitement. During one of their season games, our distinguished friend Bobby, a veteran of a referee, refrained from making a call on the opposing team that our oldest, Derek, being under the hoop, was expecting.

With the whistle announcing the next time-out, Derek sprinted over to Bobby and kindly asked him about it. Bobby gladly explained why the violation was an exception in this case to Derek, and after thanking him, Derek hurried over to join his teammates' huddle around their coach. His teammate Jake inquired curiously about the conversation he had observed with the referee since Derek is usually known more for peacemaking than causing dissension. Derek explained that he simply wanted to know the rules of the game and how Bobby had informed him.

Sitting a row up behind on the bleachers, Dave and I overheard the conversation, and we remember Jake's impressed acknowledgment of what he learned. He concluded by exclaiming, "I need to be more of an asker!" as they walked back out onto the court. I saw this fine young man with his wife in town yesterday and was inspired by the fruits that have come out of his position of teachability. It is evident that Derek and his teammate continue with an open heart of being "askers" and keeping that teach-ability, humility, and awareness of others' perspectives. Currently the teammate sits in the seat as our youngest county commissioner while Derek is our youngest man to have his own office at Gospel Express Ministries under the title of development manager.

A good question that I ask myself is, "Am I a good listener?" When I am in a conversation, am I just waiting until someone finishes talking to share my story or facts? Do I push to be understood more than I discern as they share in order to "read between the lines" so as to hear their heart for what they are really saying? Just like voice tones and body language are 70% of what a person communicates and only 30% the actual words they use, so it is when you listen well to a person. You want to hear where they are coming from in their heart and emotions when they speak words to you.

When I was young and unconverted, I remember being so impressed as I read the eyewitness accounts of the dialogue Jesus had three millennia ago with people who challenged their Creator to come in flesh. How our Savior could read people's motives before or while they even spoke! I am still His biggest fan and mark one up for Him in my head as I read how He slams His accusers with perfect antonym Truth! Though unlike our slams, His were never out of selfishness or animosity toward the person but always exposing the ugly unbelief and sin.

I hope this book is a helpful tool to assist many of us to be "more of an asker" to the next generation. Thankfully, by God's grace, we as parents have been able to give what we never got in many areas when we receive and draw out these attributes from the Divine One in us.

A Proper Apology

What to do when your child responds with specifics that have offended or affected them negatively.

It is very important that you:

1. Never defend your actions during this time, no matter how pure your motive was.
2. Keep smiling pleasantly if you want them to feel safe to always be honest with you.
3. Let them finish uninterrupted.
4. Look kindly into their face, always welcoming and softening affectionately to tears.
5. Very specifically and with mercy ask for forgiveness for what was spoken and how it made them feel, even if you had pure motives with no hurt intended.
6. Sincerely try to affirm them with positive attributes of who they are, mentioning that a negative action does not necessarily define their identity as that. Attempt to bring healing opposite words to the "unloving emotion" they had felt in the circumstance by speaking affirmation in the "unconditional, nonperformance-based love" you want them to experience from you like our Heavenly Father does to us.

7. If it was brought out that they struggle with a circumstance, try not to start in with "if I have hurt you in anyway" but rather ask if one of these that might fit :

    a. What did I say or do that was hard for you?
    b. "How did it make you feel when . . ." quoting the scenario they brought up.
    c. What did you sense from me in that scenario?
    d. What could I have done or said that would have felt loving and protecting to you in those circumstances?

8. As the responsible adult in this relationship, predetermine throughout this date no matter how they answer any questions to:

    a. Restate specifically how they described that you made them feel with your words, attitude, or actions and ask them humbly if they could find it in their heart to forgive you.
    b. Express how sorry you are for how it did affect and has affected them. But don't stay on a guilt or shame trip. They also have filters that they may receive things very differently than you intended.

Kind Confrontations

"Moreover if your brother sins against you, go and tell him his fault between you and him alone. If he hears you, you have gained your brother. But if he will not hear, take with you one or two more, that 'by the mouth of two or three witnesses every word may be established" (Matt. 18:15–16, NKJV).

When done in a humble, loving attitude, this principle for confronting anyone of offenses, including our own children, works great!

Correction in Public

"And ye Fathers, provoke not your children to wrath, but bring them up in the nurture and admonition of the Lord." Ephesians 6:4, KJV

How does one nurture and admonish in the Lord instead of provoking wrath? Here are some practical ways we have attempted to follow this pure and wise standard from God's Word. This is recommended when in private, with the family, but it is especially important when in the presence of others, both for the child's sake and that the Word of God be not blasphemed.

Responding to Public Misconduct in Preschoolers

You as the adult can kindly call the child to you or ask to lead them aside to privacy, calming and holding them or their hand. Gently, quietly ask why they did what they did in case you missed an offense done to them. Once they feel heard on anything you had not thought of or noticed, explain what is not acceptable in their behavior or response. After hearing them out, you can take this opportunity to have a clear teaching moment of what would have been the best response in the circumstance and what action you would like them to take next time.

You are redeeming an ugly situation into a beautiful teaching, bonding moment, building trust and affirmation in your child so they feel loved and not rejected.

They will feel valued that you love them enough to take time away from your friends to explain their error. This builds secure children and a trust and honor system that we found lasted beyond the teen years into adulthood.

Responding to Public Misconduct in Mature Children

1. You want to watch for an opportunity for a quiet one-on-one conversation with your child or invite them to your side and inconspicuously let them know kindly what the clear expectation would be in this circumstance.

2. Inquire why they did what they did with a question in case you missed an offense done to them. If an offense was done to them, it does not excuse their behavior but will help you coach them during step 3. This step will be on how self-control can be applied to respond to an offense rather than react. Once they feel heard about any hardships they were experiencing that you had not thought of or noticed, you are ready for step 3.

3. Next you explain to them what was not acceptable

in their behavior or response, followed by what would have been an alternative or best response in that circumstance.

4. Discern and explain what action you would like them to take now.

You are redeeming an ugly situation into a beautiful teaching, bonding moment, building trust and affirmation in your child while they feel loved and not rejected.

Responding to Negative Feedback Concerning Your Child

1. Consider the child innocent in motive, and maybe even action, until proven otherwise.
2. Discuss the information you have currently and decide together as parents on a safe, nonthreatening time and setting to kindly approach.
3. Pray for God to prepare all of your hearts ahead of time and show you the right time. Another day or week with a possible offense or secret sin on their conscience may not be worse than you blowing this special opportunity to have a conversation that could help or hinder your future heart-to-heart connection with your child.
4. If both parents have a good relationship with the child, having both genders of parents together in the meeting to discuss an intimate subject with the child can feel very reassuring.
5. Try to keep the setting comfortable, with the child between the two parents. Avoid having a child looking across at the two parents if possible. If they are comfortable with you, try having one of you close enough to put a hand on their arm or shoul-

der while the other is able to look them in the eyes when they speak.

6. Start by thanking them for their time. Ask them if there is anything in their life that they have been struggling with, that has been bothering them, or that they have been wanting to talk about with someone. Tell them you parents want to be available and walk with them through hard stages and awkward things if they let you.

7. If they don't open up and offer any information, sign of acknowledgment, or humble confession, then you may have to bring up the date or place and ask if anything happened there they would like to talk about. You can offer a testimony of your own on the subject as a confession and acknowledgment of your own moral failures. If you feel relatable and not too adult or holy, then your child will often feel safe enough to be honest.

8. The last resort is to actually tell them the information you have and ask what got them to that point of action, that you would like to hear their version of the scenario.

Your Child's Heart

They will feel valued that you love them enough to take time away from your friends to explain their error. This builds secure children and a trust and honor system that we found lasted beyond the teen years into adulthood. We do realize

that if and when our children are currently thoughtful, sensitive, and responsible leaders, it is in spite of us because of God's favor and not because we have always used this parenting formula consistently. God does honor His principles and His set law of sowing and reaping. If you sow honesty, honor, and humility now, that is mostly what you will be reaping in your future with a few exceptions and character tests here and there.

Doing Your Homework

No matter the age, asking permission to have a time for a talk ahead of time makes a person feel honored and valued as we ask if they are willing to give of their time for our relationship and communication. When they experience us giving our precious time to sit together and listen well so we both have an opportunity to communicate, it should help the bond between us if done carefully in love.

I observed that the more we as parents took time to teach at home, the less we needed to correct or explain to our children when in public. We could then simply be maintaining the same standards we had established at home.

List of Emotions

Negative Emotions:

Abandoned
Alone
Betrayed
Controlled
Deceived
Defective
Disappointment
Disconnected
Disrespected
Dumb
Failure
Helpless
Hopeless
Humiliated
Ignored
Inferior
Insignificant
Invalidated
Judged
Misportrayed
Misrepresented
Misunderstood
Not Good Enough
Phony

Pitiful
Rejected
Silly
Stupid
Taken Advantage of
Unaware
Unfair
Unimportant
Uninformed
Uninvited
Unknown
Unloved
Unwanted
Worthless

Positive Emotions:

- Accepted
- Accredited
- Accurately Portrayed
- Adequate
- Affection
- Affirmed
- Appreciated
- Approval
- Assisted
- Attention
- Cared for
- Comforted
- Companionship
- Competence
- Completeness
- Connection
- Consistent
- Content
- Creative
- Defended
- Empowered
- Enlightened
- Excited
- Fought for
- Grace
- Graceful
- Gracious
- Grateful
- Happy
- Heroic
- Hopeful
- Important
- Intimacy
- Joyful
- Kindness
- Kinship
- Laughter
- Loved
- Pampered
- Partnership
- Passion
- Peaceful
- Powerful
- Protected
- Remembered
- Respected
- Safe
- Satisfied
- Self-determined
- Serene
- Special
- Successful
- Supported
- Trusted
- Treated
- Understood
- Unique
- Useful
- Validated
- Vindicated
- Wanted

Heart Care

Deflecting praise for today's gifts and tests. Exposing where God wants to make you more whole in your soul.

Day #1: Today's Gifts

Positive emotions I experienced:

____

Whom to thank:

____

Day #1: Today's Tests

Negative emotions I experienced:

____

Whom to forgive:

____

Day #2: Today's Gifts

Positive emotions I experienced:

____

Whom to thank:

____

Day #2: Today's Tests

Negative emotions I experienced:

____

Whom to forgive:

____

See the "Why Am I Triggered" section of the index for further inward searching.

Why Am I Triggered?

What does it mean to be triggered? A certain word, phrase, or action might cause you to feel a strong emotion, positive or negative, that makes it difficult for you to respond calmly and not react. You can also be triggered when something memorable from your childhood replays. It could be a smell, sound, texture of food, song, words, or pictures that cause your heart to race, that cause happy joyous feelings or fear, that may make you feel unsafe or like hiding, running, screaming, or doing acts of violence in anger.

Where do these triggers or negative emotions come from? Past Experiences.

Steps to getting to the root of our triggers:

1. I am aware that I have been triggered and felt like reacting.

2. I acknowledge to myself, God, or someone what I am feeling is real to me, and unless attended to, I will not be a healthy me in the future.

3. Finding the root memory of lie based repetitive emotion.

    A. What is the word or phrase that best describes your emotion of how circumstance that made you feel. _______________________________________

    B. What else comes to mind as you focus on what you are feeling? _______________________________

    C. Are there other memories that come to your mind that you experienced that same feeling?

      Memory#1 ___________________________________

      Memory#2 ___________________________________

      Memory#3 ___________________________________

      Memory#4 ___________________________________

    D. And How does that make you feel?

       ____

    E. Why or when do you think you started feeling that way if people aren't always thoughtful?

       ____

    F. Why does believing _____________________

       make you feel ________________________?

4. Not that it's true, but does it feel true that . . . (embedded lie) ______________________________

    _____________________________?

5. Present <u>this belief</u> to the Lord out loud and ask Him, " Lord, what do you want me to know?"

6. Close your eyes and wait quietly before Him. No problem, if you don't hear anything right then.

    A. Keep seeking Him about it and see if the lie still feels true within a week. He may have transformed it for you for the rest of your life.

    B. Does it still feel true that (belief)

       ______________________________?

7. Truths in God's Word that would debunk the lie which I have felt is an actual fact about me. (to assist, you can search on the truth versus lies page)

    ____

Discern if it is necessary to have a kind heart-to-heart talk with the person who happened to bring out your trigger. Sometimes God wants us just to look inward and only pray for them as we process why we heard and perceived their words or actions the way we did. Did we hear or see it through a familiar filter from the past?

Personalities

As you think about the little people in your house, remind yourself that they are individually different. Frequently ask God for His wisdom to help shape them into who He created and meant for them to be in your family and society someday with their unique personality and skill set.

Through the years people have studied the various personality types using different methods. We will name some of the most used terminologies and tests available to identify an individual's strengths and weaknesses to help you understand and appreciate each person more completely.

Personality Test Types

1. The personalities have been categorized as four, five, or eight temperaments since ancient times:

2. **The Big Five** were called Extroversion, Openness, Agreeableness, Conscientiousness, and Neuroticism.

3. **The Myer-Briggs Eight** were called Introversion versus Extroversion, Sensing versus Intuition, Thinking versus Feeling, and Judging versus Perceiving.

4. **The DISC**™ personality model recognizes four behavioral types in more modern language. D stands

for Dominance, I for Influence, S for Steadiness, and C for Conscientiousness. For a free Personality Assessment by Master DISC Trainer visit http://davekaufmanspeaks.com.

5. Different temperaments that have been categorized as **The Four** are called: sanguine, choleric, melancholic, and phlegmatic. Free online test at: https://psychologia.co/four-temperaments-test/

6. Gary Smalley and John Trent also redefined the four personalities in **The Smalley Trent Personality Test** as specific animals with these characteristic tendencies. They defined the Choleric/Dominant type as a Lion™, the Sanguine/Influencer as an Otter™, the Phlegmatic/Steady type as a Golden Retriever™, and the Melancholic/Conscientious type as a Beaver™. Free online test at https://www.mint-hr.com/smalley-trent.html

7. **The Enneagram** is an old Eastern study that has been resurrected as a way to divide the personalities into categories numbered 1–9 for the dominant one and then a secondary personality number called a "wing." Although the original study may not have been done by believers, I like how it was summed up on Annie F. Downs's podcast, *That Sounds Fun*. During the marveling of the variety of personalities, it was acknowledged that "it recognizes 9 characteristics that God Himself is, that He then as Creator breaks up individually and puts into humans." Free online test: https://www.bestenneagramtest.com/enneagram-test-how-can-i-find-out-my-enneagram-type

8. The **oldest study** goes back to somewhere between 460 BC and 370 BC when Hippocrates made a medical study of the four personality traits that four bodily fluids affect and was later given the A-D descriptions by cardiologists Meyer Friedman and Ray Rosenman.

    The letters stand for:

    A. Meticulous and likes to take charge.

    B. Easygoing, relaxed, and flexible.

    C. Accurate, rational, and applying logic to everything they do.

    D. Reserved role model and distressed because of a lot of suppressed negative emotions.

For a free test go to: https://practicalpie.com/type-a-and-type-b-personalities/

Shaming A Child

Did any of you grow up reading the printed children's magazine *Highlights*™? It was started in 1946 by Garry Cleveland Myers and Caroline Clark Myers and has been printed monthly for seventy-five years. This is another way God spoke to me in what is the right and wrong way in my childhood. There was a special picture comic strip inside called Goofus and Gallant that was authored by Garry Cleveland himself and is currently being illustrated by Leslie Harrington. It made practical the saying "good is the enemy of the best." Goofus actually means foolish. The first examples below represent Goofus parents, and the second option represents Gallant parents.

I Peter 2:1–12 talks about how God will not let us come to shame because we have believed in His Son. It talks about how God has honored the Son and made Him the chief cornerstone and Great High Priest. How much like our Holy Father do we want to honor our children and give them positions and opportunities, even unmerited? Honor and responsibility normally promotes purpose, identity, and motivation to walk worthily.

There may be some exceptions to this if unhealthy and distrustful, hypocritical authorities impact a person's childhood to distort what comes natural to a trusting, innocent child in a safe environment of bonding in a healthy way. Shaming and blaming go hand in hand. Here are some alternatives to accomplish teaching the same thing with upbuilding, honoring words of life, and encouragement using a Goofus and Gallant method of comparison.

Some parenting phrases and mentalities that shame a child:

1. "If you wouldn't have ____________, then this would not be happening." vs. "It's all right, we can work with it."

2. "You cause us to ____________ because you ____________." vs. "Mother and I are very concerned but want to walk with you through this."

3. "Why don't you try to ________ more like _______ does." vs. "You children are all unique and excel in different areas."

4. "Don't you know better?" vs. "Oh, darling, it will be okay. So sorry, let's see what we can do."

5. "I would have thought you would ________ rather than ________." vs. "I want to be understanding, we all make mistakes. Did you want to talk more about it?"

6. "It is your own fault that ____________." vs. "This is a natural consequence of reaping what you sow, and I am so sorry."

7. "I don't understand why you don't learn ________." vs. "Is this a test or something you have faced before?"

8. "I told you so." vs. "I want to be patient and remember how I was at your age and give grace."

9. "If you could only remember to ________." vs. "I pray God will help you remember to ________."

10. "How could you be so _______." vs. "I am so glad you are ________, and I was sorry to hear that you ____________."

11. "You will never _______ if you ________." vs. "I am trusting God will help you to be _______ someday as you grow and learn through hard things."

12. "Try and be more _______ next time." vs. "I pray you can use this as a step up for the next time and God will help you to not go there again."

Possible Reasons
for Rebellion or Shut Down

*Fathers, do not provoke your children, lest
they become discouraged.*
Colossians 3:21, ESV

*And ye Fathers, provoke not your children to
wrath, but bring them up in the nurture and
admonition of the Lord.*
Ephesians 6:4, KJV

How might we be discouraging or provoking them to
wrath?

Adopted or Foster Children

Adopted or foster children who
are grieving the rejection felt
from the absence of their bio-
logical parents may resist even
the kindest, best parents who
choose them while battling
so many emotional, identity,
and trust factors in this confusion. Getting experienced, biblical
counselors and advisers involved
is invaluable for both the parents
and the children as they process
bonding and resisting difficulties that cause many misunderstandings and
hurt both parties as the child grows.

Provoking a Child

I find it interesting how God led the apostle Paul to bring out two different points in the different letters to each region, after he gave the command to the believing fathers.

To the Colossians, he gives the predicted results if they do provoke them to anger. "Fathers, do not provoke your children, lest they become discouraged" (Col. 3:21, ESV.

Provoking or Nurturing?

To the church at Ephesus, he tells them what they can do—the opposite of provoking them to anger! "And ye Fathers, provoke not your children to wrath, but bring them up in the nurture and admonition of the Lord" (Eph. 6:4, KJV).

I am so happy he mentions nurture and teaching together! Not only did he mention nurture first, but what kind of nurture? The nurture of our Lord Jesus? What kind is that? Have you experienced Jesus's nurture in your life? I have. It is gentle and kind.

I was raised by a dear mother who hardly experienced any nurture at all during her childhood. As we travel the world and listen to people's stories, I have come to realize even the basic provision and teaching that my mother received is more than many children in the world ever get when born into very depraved, devastating, or dark circumstances.

When I surrendered my life to God, believing in Jesus as my Savior at nineteen years old, I began the journey to get to know the Heavenly Father. When we realize the huge allegory of how we experience the adults and authorities in our life as a child and how it has affected our view of

God, we start processing our past. We would all do well to stop and grieve what we never had from earthly parents that God may have intended when He made man and his companion, the woman, for each other, and they are to be one flesh and replenish the earth (Matt. 19:4–6).

We all can do this without putting any blame on anyone, knowing we have not always shown the Father perfectly to others ourselves. Thank God our children and people we influence have access to Jesus's healing and grace just like we have for our wholeness if nurturing waned in our childhood.

These are verses that are really good to look up in your quiet time on your phone and read them to yourself in various translations. It brings the overall meaning home.

This link https://www.biblesumo.com/ways-parents-provoke-children-anger/amp/ leads you to a very good study brother Pedro Cheung did on this verse. He wrote a practical twelve-minute read on twelve ways we could be provoking our children totally unawares.

Here are twenty ways that could contribute:

1. Neglect time with your child
2. Model sinful anger
3. Correcting a child in anger without apologizing
4. Speaking constant correction with very little affirmation
5. Not hearing the child's heart
6. Having no safe boundaries and too much loose freedom
7. Being hard or impossible to please with high demands
8. Living double standards or changing them

9. Comparing your child to others
10. Not carrying out promises or hints of rewards
11. Humiliating your child in public
12. Having favorites or injustices
13. Not respecting both parents of the child
14. Bribing the child into obedience
15. Using passive-aggressive comments, guilt trips, or threats for obedience
16. Not treating their privacy, things, or feelings with respect
17. Speaking negatively about them to your or their friends.
18. Embarrassing or shaming them in front of others
19. Taking advantage of them or their things
20. Any dishonesty, perversion, or selfishness without you acknowledging it

Biblical Warnings to Guide Us

1. "Pride goeth before destruction and an haughty spirit before a fall." Proverbs 16:18, KJV.
2. "God resisteth the proud but giveth grace unto the humble." James 4:6b, KJV
3. "For I the Lord, they God am a jealous God visiting the Iniquities of the Fathers upon the children unto the third and fourth generation of them that hate me." Deuteronomy 5:9 KJV
4. "Hope deferred maketh the heart sick . . ." Proverbs 13:12a, KJV
5. "Fathers Provoke not to wrath...lest they be discouraged." (Col. 3:21, ESV.

Selfish parenting often equals children not desiring to place their parents as a priority when they are older. Rules without relationships reap rebellion, or at the least, a sad heart needing healing.

We reap what we sow. Priorities are caught rather than taught. Is my reputation more important than my children's feelings? Have I dishonored, belittled, and scolded my children in front of other people to make myself look good and make my child the problem? Our children will do the same back to us when they are adults unless they choose mercy toward our offenses and secret sin.

Gospel Answer Key

Answers for the theological questions for the "Gospel Dates."

Preschool, Date 7: Gospel Answer Key

Question 1. God spoke it into being around 6,000 years ago. According to studies of Genesis.

1 In the beginning God created the heavens and the earth.

2 And the earth was without form, and void; and darkness was upon the face of the deep. And the Spirit of God moved upon the face of the waters.

3 And God said, Let there be light: and there was light.

4 And God saw the light, that it was good: and God divided the light from the darkness.

5 And God called the light Day, and the darkness he called Night. And the evening and the morning were the first day.

6 And God said, Let there be a firmament in the midst of the waters, and let it divide the waters from

11 And God said, Let the earth bring forth grass, the herb yielding seed, and the fruit tree yielding fruit after his kind, whose seed is in itself, upon the earth: and it was so.

12 And the earth brought forth grass, and herb yielding seed after his kind, and the tree yielding fruit, whose seed was in itself, after his kind: and God saw that it was good.

Question 2. God made us and all the trees and plants.

> 26 And God said, Let us make man in our image, after our likeness: and let them have dominion over the fish of the sea, and over the fowl of the air, and over the cattle, and over all the earth, and over every creeping thing that creepeth upon the earth.
>
> 27 So God created man in his own image, in the image of God created he him; male and female created He them. Genesis 1:26–27, KJV.
>
> "For by him were all things created, that are in heaven, and that are in earth, visible and invisible, whether they be thrones, or dominions, or principalities, or powers: all things were created by him, and for him: and he is before all things, and by him all things consist." Colossians 1:16–20, KJV

Question 3. Adam and Eve found in Gen. 2:20 and Gen 3:20.

Question 4. God saw that it was Good. Gen 1:12

Question 5. They were free to eat from any tree in the garden except for the Tree of the Knowledge of Good and Evil. Gen 2:17

Question 6. The Tree of the Knowledge of Good and Evil. Gen 2:17

Question 7. Once they eat from it, they would certainly die. Gen 2:17

Question 8. The serpent. Gen 3:1

Question 9. "Eve saw that the fruit was good for food, pleasing to look at and desirable for gaining wisdom. Next Eve took some, ate it and gave some to her husband." Gen 3:6

Question 10. Sin. Gen 4:7

Elementary, Date 4: Gospel Answer Key

1. Answers will vary with each child.
2. B
3. A
4. D
5. A Rev 20:4
6. And on down, the answers will vary with each child.

The Miller Family

Family Instagram:
Miller.family7

Ruthann Instagram:
ruthannmiller1971

Gospel Express Facebook:
Gospel Express
Evangelistic Team
Ministry

Ruthann Facebook:
Ruth Ann Miller

*Corbin, Deborah &
Porter Borkholder*

Latest Miller Family Albums
Music also available on all digital platforms.
Search: The Millers

Daughter
*by Deborah Isabel
(Miller) Borkholder*

Dave Miller Sermons

For links and to order any
of these resources, visit:

Gospelexpress.com/Gladyouasked

or scan the QR Code